English Progress

Pupil Book 1

Series editor: **Geoff Barton**
Series consultant: **Michael Jones**

Authors:
Geoff Barton
Bernadette Carroll
Clare Constant
Emma Lee
Michele Paule
Alan Pearce

PEARSON
Longman

Contents

Writing

Get ready for English Progress!

The purpose of the book

This book is designed to help you to boost your levels and accelerate the progress you make in English. Why is it important to make progress in English? The skills you develop in this subject improve your ability to communicate effectively and understand the world around you. Making progress up the levels in English is not just important for this subject, but can also help your learning in other subjects too.

How the book is structured

English Progress is divided into three sections covering the three main skills you use in the subject of English as well as in your everyday life:

Speaking and Listening

Reading

Writing

Each section is divided into individual units which focus on a specific area of reading, writing or speaking and listening. Each unit covers the essential skills that you need to develop to make progress and improve your level in that area of English. These units are organised around the Assessment Focuses which are used in tests at Key Stage 3.

For example, **Writing Unit AF4** *Progress in ... using paragraphs to make ideas clear* helps you to improve the way you use paragraphs to organise your writing and link your ideas.

At the end of each of the three sections is an **Assessing your Progress** unit. This gives you the opportunity to check your overall progress in either reading, writing or speaking and listening and see what level you are currently working at. These units help you to see which areas you are doing well in, which areas you still need to improve in and to set targets to help you move to the next level.

Climb the levels with English Progress

Every unit follows the same structure to help you to build your learning and focus on the progress you need to make. The diagram opposite shows you how to use the units to make progress.

What are you going to learn?

Learning objectives explain the skills you will be focusing on in the unit.

What can you already do?

Activate your learning gets you thinking about the area in focus. **Assess to Progress** lets you show what skills you already have. Your teacher will give you a **progression ladder** to help you set targets to improve your level.

How can you make progress?

Build your skills models the skills you need to develop to make progress. **Skills tutorials** on the ActiveTeach support you in developing these skills and you can refer to these when working independently.

Try it yourself

Reinforce your skills and **Extend your skills** allow you to try out the skills you are developing. Your teacher might suggest that you look at the **Support** boxes, which will give you extra help, or the **Stretch** boxes, which set you additional challenges.

Show what you can do now

Apply your learning is a task that gives you an opportunity to put all you have learned together. **Skills for Life** allows you to show how you would use functional skills in a real-world situation.

Check your progress

Assess to progress allows you to check the progress you have made and set targets for future improvement. Now is the time to look again at your **progression ladder**.

What can you do to improve?

To keep developing your skills further, use your **progression ladder** to set yourself targets. Use the **skills tutorials** if you need to revise the strategies that you learned in this unit.

Progress in ...
Speaking and Listening

Speaking and Listening AF1
Progress in ... Making talk interesting for listeners

LEARNING OBJECTIVES ⭐

- Use verbal and non-verbal techniques to make talk interesting for listeners.
- Use voice for expression and emphasis.
- Use body language to help keep your listeners' attention.

Activate your learning

1 In groups of four, you have one minute to say each of the four phrases below in as many ways as you can. See how many different ways you can come up with in order to change the way you say these simple words. For instance, you could:

- emphasise a particular word
- add a pause for emphasis
- turn it into a question
- add emotion.

> Pass the salt.

> I'm sorry.

> Don't try and stop me.

> I love sherbet lemons.

2 In your group, discuss these questions:

- What effect does the way you say a phrase have on the meaning of what you say?
- Why do you think people change the emphasis of what they say?

3 Work in a group of four. Each of you will retell a story, for example, *The Three Little Pigs* or *Anansi*. You may like to pretend that you are telling the story to young children.

When you are telling your story, make sure you:

- look directly at the audience
- don't speak too quickly
- pause at certain points for effect
- use your hands and your face to express feelings
- use gestures to involve the audience or emphasise parts of the story.

Assess to Progress

Now decide how good you are at each of the following speaking skills. Think about the storytelling activity you have just done, as well as other times when you have tried to make what you say interesting, for example when:

- trying to encourage people to listen to you
- speaking to an unfamiliar audience
- presenting a point of view and trying to convince your listeners
- keeping listeners', attention when giving a formal presentation.

☹ means you find this skill hard, ☺ means you feel you are already good at this skill, and ☺ means you still think you need to develop this skill more.

	☹	☺	☺
Telling a story in a way that interests the audience			
Giving clear answers, instructions or explanations			
Sharing your ideas and feelings			
Presenting information or a point of view clearly and in appropriate language			
Using your voice well, e.g. to emphasise words, express feelings			
Using body language (e.g. hands, face) to make your talk clear and effective			

Build your skills

This unit focuses on using verbal and non-verbal techniques to make what you say interesting for listeners. Below, a teenager is telling a scary story to friends at a sleepover party.

1 Read the comments on the first part of the story. These describe how the storyteller uses different verbal and non-verbal techniques, such as words, voice and body language, to engage the audience's attention. Notice that the storyteller:

- changes his voice to alter the pace

- uses different voices for the characters, and to bring out their feelings

- uses his face, arms and hands to add expression

- keeps eye contact with the audience.

The speaker emphasises the words 'miserable' and 'wet', pausing between them to allow the listeners to imagine the scene.

> It was a <u>miserable</u>, <u>wet</u> night in the middle of November. Mark and Tracy were trying hard to get home as fast as they could. Their car windscreen was <u>misted over</u>, and the rain was pelting down, making it hard to see even a few metres in front of them.

The speaker moves his hands in front of his face when he says 'misted over' to show that the characters couldn't see.

The speaker uses a different voice to show that the newsreader is speaking.

> Mark turned the radio on to keep them company as they drove along. Suddenly the music was interrupted by a local news bulletin: '<u>... on the run from Huntsmoor Prison. Do not approach this man. He is armed and extremely dangerous...</u>'

The speaker keeps eye contact with his audience. This holds their attention.

The speaker shows in his face and voice that Tracy is nervous.

> 'Wow, Huntsmoor is round here, isn't it?' asked Tracy <u>nervously</u>.
>
> That was the moment they lost radio contact. There was nothing but static.

The speaker pauses dramatically here for effect. He also speaks more slowly, emphasising each word in the next sentence.

2 Here is the next part of the story. Discuss with a partner how you could narrate this section effectively and try it out. Which words will you emphasise? Check that you are using your voice and body language effectively.

> 'Damn! That's just our luck,' said Mark. 'We're stuck in a rainstorm with no radio contact and a mass murderer on the loose.' He gave a wicked chuckle.
>
> Then, out of the darkness, there he was ...

Reinforce your skills

In pairs, you are now going to finish telling the scary story. Then you will give feedback to your partner on their performance.

1   Discuss with a partner how this story might end. Here is one possibility:

    The man pulls Mark out of the car. He drives off into the night, with Tracy still in the car. A shot is heard.

2   Still in pairs, take it in turns to finish telling the story. Remember to focus on your tone of voice, eye contact, body language and pace.

3   Give feedback to your partner about how well they told the story. The following questions might help you to give comments:

   • How much did they use eye contact?

   • What did you notice about their gestures?

   • Did they vary the pace, use pauses and emphasise particular words?

   • What did they do really well?

   • What change could they make that would improve their speaking skills the most?

Support

When you are listening to your partner telling their story, make some notes to help you give feedback later:
• Note one thing that you like about the way they use their **voice**. Then note one thing that doesn't work so well. How could they improve it?
• Note one thing that you like about their **body language**. Then note one thing that doesn't work so well. How could they improve it?

Stretch

Use the feedback you are given to identify two things you could improve. Retell part of the story and try to focus on these areas. Do you notice any difference in your partner's reaction?

Extend your skills

You are going to work in pairs to make a short presentation about what you think makes an interesting speaker. You should show your audience how to be a good speaker, demonstrating and explaining the skills you think they need.

1   Make a list of the skills you think an interesting speaker should have. For each one, decide how to demonstrate it to the audience. For example, how could you demonstrate using eye contact effectively?

2   Think of two specific examples of skills that you have used in the activities earlier in this unit. Include these in your presentation to show what skills you have developed in this unit.

3   Practise making your presentation before you share it with the rest of your class. Remember, you need to demonstrate all of the skills that you think are important as you make your presentation!

Apply your learning

Task   Working on your own, you are going to tell a story from the point of view of a **villain**. This could be a fairy story or folk tale, or you may like to retell the scary story you worked on earlier.

Try to include some explanation of why you acted as you did. You should try to persuade the audience that you didn't really do anything wrong, and it is vital that you keep their interest! Here are some possibilities:

- *Jack and the Beanstalk* retold from the point of view of the giant.

- *Shrek (The Third)* retold from the point of view of Prince Charming.

Remember to:

- vary the volume of your voice and the speed of your sentences

- get eye contact with your listeners

- use body language and expression to show your feelings.

Assess to Progress

Complete the statements below to help you identify your skills in making talk interesting for listeners and areas you need to develop. Make reference to the following skills:

- Alternating the pace of my speech and using pauses.

- Using my voice to add emphasis to particular words or phrases.

- Using body language and eye contact to keep the audience's attention.

If your teacher has recorded your performance, you can also use this to help you evaluate your performance.

When I told the first story I ...

What I really worked on in this unit was ...

So I have improved in the following area ...

Things I can do to improve even more are ...

Now return to the grid that you filled in at the beginning of the unit on page 3. This evaluated your speaking skills in general. Can you change any of the ratings you gave yourself?

SKILLS FOR LIFE

You and a friend have applied to work at a children's activity camp during the holidays. The organiser is looking for volunteers to entertain the youngest children with stories.

Working with a partner, role-play an interview with the organiser, explaining how you would entertain the children. You should:

- explain why you would be a good person to work at the activity camp

- use body language and eye contact to keep the interviewer interested in what you are saying

- demonstrate your skills by showing how you would read the opening of a fairy story in a way that would keep very young children interested and entertained.

Progress in ... Listening and responding

LEARNING OBJECTIVES ⭐

- Understand why someone is speaking and what points they are making.
- Pick out and summarise the key ideas from what a speaker says.
- Identify how speakers use tone to show their feelings or points of view.

Activate your learning

1 You are going to listen carefully to two different speakers. After each one finishes speaking, complete the relevant column in a copy of the chart below. This will show how well you understood what was being said.

	Ship's captain	Woman on phone
What are the speaker's main ideas?		
What is the speaker's purpose? e.g. to persuade, explain, inform		
What is the speaker's opinion about what has happened?		
What is the speaker feeling as s/he speaks? e.g. angry, excited		

2   What do you need to do if you are going to listen well? Look at each of the suggestions in the list below and decide whether each one is an example of good or poor listening skills. Be prepared to give your reasons.

- Interrupting the person speaking.

- Trying to follow what is being said in your mind.

- Hearing every word the speaker says.

- Daydreaming or chatting to someone else while someone is speaking.

- Thinking about what the other person is telling you.

- Replying using something that has been said to begin with, e.g. 'When you said...'.

- Looking at the person speaking and noticing the way they are talking and how they look.

- Saying whatever you want whenever you want to say it.

- Knowing what you want to find out while you are listening to the speaker.

Assess to Progress

How good are your listening skills already? Think about the task you have just done, as well as other situations you can remember. For each skill in the list below give yourself a score ranging from 1 (I find this difficult) to 7 (I'm good at this).

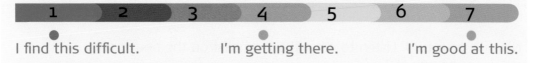

| 1 | 2 | 3 | 4 | 5 | 6 | 7 |

I find this difficult.   I'm getting there.   I'm good at this.

- When I listen to someone's speech I can spot their main points, purpose and opinions.

- I can recognise the speaker's feelings from the way they speak, e.g. happy, sad, angry.

- I can comment on the points a speaker has made, e.g. It sounds as if you've already arranged a lift there.

- After listening carefully to what the speaker has to say I can respond by asking sensible questions, e.g. Saturday is no good. How about going on Friday night instead?

Build your skills

Step 1   Identifying the main points

Ryan is watching a newsclip about a shipwreck. To work out what the speaker's main points are, he listens out for the words that tell him:

- Where
- When
- What
- Who
- How
- Why

1   Read this transcript of the newsclip and identify which words Ryan could pick out to help him identify the main points.

Where

> Now, thousands of people have been combing a beach in **Devon** today, taking away items washed ashore from the stranded container ship, the *Napoli*. Ignoring warnings from police, they took away lots of things, including rolls of carpet and boxes of shoes and motorbikes. The coastguard now says 103 containers have fallen into the water. The police are now threatening to seal off the beach tomorrow.

Ryan then tries to sum up what the speaker is saying in his own words.

> So, there's been a shipwreck in Devon and a lot of valuable cargo has come onto the beach. Locals are picking it up.

2   Now it's your turn. Listen to what the journalist on the beach says, then sum up what he says in your own words.

Step 2   Identifying the speaker's purpose and viewpoint

To work out why the speaker is talking (their **purpose**) Ryan thinks about what he has just heard and asks these questions:

- Who is the speaker? A newsreader.
- Why is the speaker telling me this? He is informing me about a shipwreck.

- What is the speaker's point of view? That some people see this disaster as an opportunity for them to grab some valuable things.

- How does the speaker sound while he is speaking? The journalist sounds calm and is being very factual.

1   Ask yourself the same four questions about what the journalist on the beach says to work out what his purpose and viewpoint are.

Step 3   Responding and commenting

You can show that you have been listening carefully to someone by asking them sensible questions about what they have just said. Their answers will help you to understand what they mean even more clearly.

Ryan thought of some questions he would like to ask the newsreader about the news report.

- **What did you mean when you said** 'the police are threatening to seal off the beach'?

   Starting a question like this helps you to ask the speaker to explain more clearly what they meant.

- **Why do you think** the police haven't done that before now?

   Starting a question like this helps you to ask a speaker to give reasons for the thoughts and opinions they have just told you.

1   Write down two questions you would like to ask the journalist on the beach, asking him to explain:

   - something he said in more detail

   - his opinion of something.

Once you understand what someone means, you can then comment on what they have said. Notice how Ryan thinks about what he has heard before making his comment.

> What do I think about the points the speaker is making?
>
> Do I agree/disagree? Why?
>
> It must be awful for the people who owned the motor bikes to have them taken away.

2   What comment can you make about what the journalist on the beach says?

Reinforce your skills

It is important to listen to the words someone says, but the way that they say them can also tell you a lot.

1   In groups, play Guess the Tone.

a) Brainstorm a list of different tones of voice people can speak in, e.g. happy, sad, angry, bored, serious.

b) Take it in turns to pick one of the tones of voice. You have to speak in that tone for 30 seconds about how you should spend five million pounds.

c) Everyone else has to listen and guess what tone of voice the speaker is using and explain how they can tell, e.g. His tone is angry because he is shouting and waving his arms around and speaking very fast.

2   You are working as journalists for *The Daily Gossip* newspaper when the story of the shipwrecked boat comes in from a news agency. Your editor wants the story to go on the front page. Use the skill steps you have just learnt to help you carry out the task below.

a) Listen to the newsclip.

- Jot down the main points that the front page needs to include.

- Decide how the Devon Wildlife Trust representative feels about the disaster. How can you tell?

b) What other information would you like to find out before writing your front page? Make a list of five questions your reporter should ask people on the beach.

Extend your skills

Work in groups of four and divide into two pairs to complete the task below.

Pair A's task:

Discuss what should be put on the newspaper's front page to grab the readers' attention and make them want to buy it. Make sure you talk about:

● what your viewpoint is going to be, e.g. lucky looters or pity for wildlife

● which of the photographs opposite will go with the article

● what would be a really effective, attention-grabbing headline

● what information you will put in the article and what you will leave out.

> ## Support
> Remember to:
> • listen to the main points your partner is making
> • be ready to comment on what your partner has said
> • ask your partner relevant questions.

Pair B's task:

Watch pair A and think about how they listen to and respond to each other while they do the task. You are going to give feedback to pair A using the questions below after they have finished their discussion.

● How well does each speaker listen to the other person?

● Does each person ask the other sensible questions about what they have just said?

● Does each person make sensible comments on what the other person said?

● What different tones of voice does each person use when they are speaking?

> ## Support
> Name one tone of voice each speaker used, e.g. calm, angry, worried.

> ## Stretch
> Suggest one way each person can improve their listening or commenting skills. Include this in your feedback, e.g. Perhaps you could try ... when you ...

Apply your learning

Task The scene at the beach has changed dramatically. People from all over Britain have driven down to Devon and are stealing as much as they can. There are ugly scenes and the police have been called. Your editor has seen the front page you've come up with and wants to talk to you. Listen to what he has to say and answer the questions below.

Kill that front page. Kill it! It's got to be completely redone. Why are we still carrying that? It's old news now. We've got to get the story of the crime that's going on there and we've got to get it done before deadline. Tomorrow morning, while all the other front pages are still bleating on about poor little birds I want *The Daily Gossip* leading the field – photos of the gangs, litter, pollution. It's a scandal. This is Britain's only National Heritage Site and look what these looters have done to it. Look at that litter, the pollution. It's the middle of the night in January and there are toddlers sat on the beach wearing T-shirts while their parents scavenge. It's a disgrace! What is this country coming to?

That's our front page story. Now let's get on with it.

1. What are the editor's main points?

2. What is his purpose in speaking?

3. What is he feeling? How can you tell?

4. Does the editor's tone change during the speech? If so, when? How?

5. Think about the tone of voice he uses at the beginning of his speech. Discuss why an editor might use that tone of voice to the journalists in this situation.

6. What other speaking skills and strategies does the editor use? What is the effect of these?

7. What is the editor's point of view?

8. Discuss what you need to find out in order to be able to produce a front page that will please him.

Assess to Progress

How good are you now at:

● Showing you have understood why someone is speaking.

● Summarising the key points from what a speaker says.

● Working out what someone is feeling from their tone of voice.

Look back at the original ratings you gave yourself at the beginning of this unit. Now decide how well you did in the activity on page 14. Rate yourself again on the scale for these skills:

a) When I listened to the editor I could work out ...

● the main points he was making

● why he was speaking (what his purpose was)

● what his thoughts and opinions were.

b) I was able to notice the editor's tone of voice.

| 1 | 2 | 3 | 4 | 5 | 6 | 7 |

I find this difficult.   I'm getting there.   I'm good at this.

SKILLS FOR LIFE

You have been asked to organise a class visit to a place of interest within 50 miles of your school. This is a reward for a good year's work. Your tutor has asked each pupil to nominate one place that they would recommend (e.g. a theme park, zoo, museum). Each person has 30 seconds to make their case, saying (a) where you would like to go, and (b) why you think it would be a good venue.

Listen to all of the recommendations and respond to each one by:

▧ asking a question which shows some interest, e.g. Have you been there before? What does it offer for our age group?

▧ listening for key words and phrases that will help you to remember the key points

▧ asking a question about the practical issues, e.g. opening times, transport there, lunch arrangements.

Progress in ... Developing speaking skills in formal and informal situations

Activate your learning

Knowing when to use the right style of speech to suit the listener is crucial to speaking effectively and appropriately.

1   Look at each of the following situations in pairs. First read each speech as it is. Then discuss how you would change the speech so that it is more appropriate for the audience. Think about both the vocabulary used and how the speaker has organised what they say.

a) You have to persuade your form group to take part in a sponsored event for WaterAid, which helps the world's poorest people to have clean water.

Well, Mrs Johnson asked me to tell you about this charity that she wants us to do something for. Ummm, they give water to kids who don't have clean water, and, umm, we could do something to get some money for them. I was thinking we could do a sponsored silence, 'cos all of you lot are dead chatty and I think a lot of people would sponsor us to keep our mouths shut for the day. Especially my mum. She'd give me loads of money just to keep me quiet!

b) A visitor to the school stops you to ask the way to reception and to talk to you about what you think about the school.

Just go down across the yard in front of the school. There's a big sign there that says 'reception'. It's pretty big. Anyway, there might be some kids there who will tell you if you can't see it.

D'you know what? I'll just take you across. You might get lost.

Our school's alright I guess. I like science lessons. Mrs Pilling is a cool teacher. She's funny and a bit crazy. She's always trying to make us sing songs and that... don't like the way it starts so early. St Peter's don't start til nine and they get to have a lie-in.

Assess to Progress

How easy did you find the activity? If you found any of the skills listed below easy, place yourself in the ☺ column. If you found it difficult, use the ☹ column. Use the ☺ column if you found it fairly straightforward, but you think you could improve.

Skills	☹	☺	☺
Picking the right words for the listener			
Giving enough detail to help the listener			
Organising what you say so that it makes sense to the listener			
Choosing the right level of formality			

Try and pick out examples of any skills you found easy. How did what you already know about these types of speech help you with this activity?

Build your skills

When you speak in different situations, it is important to think about what you are trying to say and who you are speaking to. This will help you to choose the right level of formality. **Informal** language is the type of language you would be more likely to use with your friends and might include slang words, lots of contractions (e.g. can't, won't) and fillers (e.g. like, innit).

1 Look at the following situation in which a resident of Manchester gives directions to a visitor to the town, explaining where they should go for a meal. Before you begin to read, discuss with a partner what type of language you would expect to be used in this situation.

2 Once you have read the conversation, look at the annotations to see whether the type of language you expected to see was used.

> The visitor is choosing more formal language to encourage the resident to help them out.

> The resident uses some informal words but still makes sure that the information is clear.

> The resident repeats a few details so that the visitor can recall the main information.

> The resident uses imperative verbs at the start of sentences.

Visitor: Sorry to bother you … we've just got here from London and we <u>were wondering</u> where the best place would be to get something to eat tonight. <u>You couldn't help us, could you?</u>

Resident: <u>Sure</u>! Manchester's got <u>loads</u> of different types of restaurant, and all different prices too. Some of the best chefs work here! If you want <u>Chinese</u> or oriental food, China Town is <u>fantastic</u>. It's basically a square surrounded by about fifty different restaurants. There's <u>Chinese</u> food, Japanese and Thai. If you fancy a <u>curry</u>, Rusholme is <u>great</u>. It's called '<u>Curry Mile</u>' round here, so you get an idea of how many restaurants there are there. There's some <u>award-winners</u> too. Anything take your fancy?

Visitor: Wow! It's hard to make a choice! I'd quite like some Japanese food, actually. Where'd you recommend?

Resident: Tokyo City is brilliant. It's right in the centre of Manchester. It's a bit difficult to spot though, if you don't know what you're looking for. Shall I give you directions?

Visitor: Sure!

Resident: <u>Walk</u> straight down here, Market Street, until you get to the big sign at the bottom that says Food Court. When you go under the Food Court, turn left and walk straight up until you hit the Town Hall and the square. You'll see a huge building on your left, with fountains in front of it. Keep going across the square and you'll see a block of Victorian buildings opposite. They look a bit like banks. <u>Go</u> straight over, and you'll see the sign for Tokyo City. It's in the basement, so you can't see anything from the street apart from the sign.

> The resident uses persuasive words and phrases to describe the best places to eat.

> The resident has organised what they are saying to give a bit of detail about each area: oriental food first, then curries so that the visitor doesn't get confused.

> The resident gives directions in the right order so the visitor can imagine where they need to go.

3 In pairs, role-play a similar situation, set in your home town or a town near you. Make sure you:

- choose the right level of formality
- organise the information you want to give so that it is easy to understand
- choose the right words to make your directions helpful.

Reinforce your skills

Effective speakers can change the formality of the way they speak according to the situation. To do this it is important to know how to change your language to suit different situations or audiences.

1 Read the following extract from a conversation between a group of friends discussing how they spent their Saturday afternoon.

Non-standard subject–verb agreement

Slang expressions

Contraction

We had a laugh. Six of us was hangin' around town, just chillin', when we saw this fit guy but he was with a real minger. Dionne went over, all smiles, and fit guy thought, I'm in! But Dionne ain't interested and starts chattin' up the minger. He gets all embarrassed and the fit guy can't work out what the hell is goin' on – he wasn't used to being ignored was he! But Dionne couldn't keep it up. She gave it away when she burst out laughing and ran back to us.

2 Where would you place this conversation on the formality scale?

1 2 3 4 5 6 7

Informal   Formal

3 Some of the features of the conversation that show its informality have already been picked out for you. Working with a partner, pick out some more examples.

4 With your partner, choose one of the following situations and create two role plays.

- The first role play should be a bad example showing someone who has chosen the wrong style of speech for the situation, e.g. using slang words and phrases in a formal situation or getting their speech in the wrong order.

- The second role play should be a good example showing someone who has chosen the right style of speech for the situation.

> A head teacher talking to new parents at Open Evening, informing them about the school.

> A bank company worker phoning homes to ask if the owners would be interested in a loan.

> An older brother, aged 11, helping his little brother, aged 2, get dressed.

> A child thanking an elderly aunt, who they don't know very well, for a present.

> Two teenage girls shopping on a Saturday afternoon, discussing the things they've seen.

> A car sales representative persuading a customer to buy the more expensive model of the car they want.

Support

Use what you know about the type of speech used in your chosen situation to help you. For example, how would a sales person usually speak to a customer?

Stretch

Write a brief commentary on your role plays describing the differences between the good and bad examples.

Extend your skills

TV and radio presenters have to make sure that they use the right style of speech to fit their purpose and appeal to the audience they expect to be listening.

The purpose of a news report is to give the listener information about what is happening in a clear and objective (unbiased and not emotional) way. In a news report it is important to:

● choose the right vocabulary to make information clear

● structure the report so that readers can follow the information.

News reports often use the passive voice where the object of the verb is turned into a subject and put at the beginning of a sentence to focus on the result of the action. For example, a news report would say 'A man has been arrested' instead of 'Police have arrested a man.'

1   Working in a group of four, listen to two different radio news reports, for example Radio 1's *Newsbeat* and the lunchtime news on Radio 2. Think about the different audiences the reports are aimed at and how the presenters speak in ways that appeal to their listeners.

2   Copy and complete the following chart as you listen to the bulletins again.

	News bulletin 1	News bulletin 2
What are the news items about? List them briefly.		
How are the news items organised? Which story comes first? Which comes last?		
What type of language does the presenter use? Is it more formal or are some informal words and phrases used? Give examples.		
Does the report use the passive voice?		

3   Working in your group, compare the notes you have made. Discuss what similarities the two news reports have and what the main differences are.

4   Complete the following diagram. In the outer part of the circles, include things that are only in that news bulletin. In the overlapping centre section, add everything that is the same. Think about:

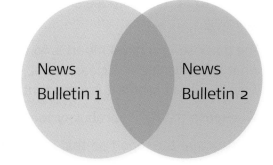

- the content

- the way they speak.

Apply your learning

Task   1   Working in pairs, you are going to create two short radio news reports for different radio stations. You need to show that you can choose the right speaking style for the audience listening to each station. Both news reports should include the following information, presenting it in a way that is suitable for the station's audience:

- Obesity among teenagers is on the rise.

- Teenagers spend increasing amounts of time at their computers or TV sets.

- The Government is spending money on sports and activities, at school and in the community.

- The London 2012 Olympics may also inspire more young people to take up sport.

Remember to use the right vocabulary to make the information in your news reports clear and think about how you structure what you say.

2   If possible, record your broadcast, using a script or notes to support you, as real news presenters do. Remember that you need to sound confident and fluent.

3   Listen to your performance before you submit it to your teacher for assessment. Check that you can spot the differences in style and formality between the two broadcasts.

Assess to Progress

How good do you think you are now at using your speaking skills in different formal and informal situations? Go back to the grid you filled in at the start of this unit and rate yourself again. Think about all the activities you have completed in this unit.

Skills	☹	😐	🙂
Picking the right words for the listener			
Giving enough detail to help the listener			
Organising what you say so that it makes sense to the listener			
Choosing the right level of formality			

With a partner, discuss which different speaking situations you are now more confident in. Which do you think you still need to improve?

SKILLS FOR LIFE

You are the volunteer manager of a school football or netball team. The team has got off to a bad start this season and you think they aren't taking the matches seriously. They aren't turning up on time to training; aren't working as a team; and aren't getting themselves in good shape by eating well, getting enough sleep, or exercising properly. Give them a team talk in which you calmly but firmly tell them your thoughts. You should:

- try to motivate the team to see what they could be like if they followed your advice, as well as criticising them

- address the team directly (e.g. 'You're all potentially good players ...')

- use connectives like 'but' and 'however' to link contrasting ideas.

Progress in ... Group discussion and interaction

LEARNING OBJECTIVES

- Make clear and relevant contributions in group discussions.
- Contribute to a discussion in different ways.
- Help discussions succeed by acknowledging and responding to what others say.

Activate your learning

Work in a group of four. Split the group into pairs and take it in turns to complete the tasks below.

1 One pair should discuss which TV programmes you would place first, second, third and fourth in a list of the **Top 100 TV programmes**.

2 a) The other pair should listen to the discussion and complete a tick chart like the one below. Give a speaker a tick each time you notice them using one of the skills.

   b) Afterwards, discuss which skills you saw each member of the group demonstrating best. Give reasons for your thoughts,

   e.g. Anna was best at being relevant because ...

Skills	Name:	Name:
Responding to what someone has just said.		
Saying something relevant (that fits in with what is being discussed).		
Being respectful to the other person's ideas, even if the speaker disagrees with them.		
Making a suggestion.		
Asking a question.		

Assess to Progress

How well can you contribute to group discussions already?

Use what you learned about yourself while taking part in the discussion to help you rank yourself for each of the skills below.

1	2	3	4	5	6	7

I find this difficult.　　I'm getting there.　　I'm good at this.

- I listen carefully to make sure that what I have to say is about what the group is talking about.
- I know when it is the right time for me to join in and how to show that I want to speak.
- I show by the way I speak and behave that I respect the other people in the group and their right to think differently to me.
- I know how to contribute to a discussion in different ways, e.g. questioning, opposing.

Build your skills

You are going to take part in a group discussion about the viewing schedule for **TopTV** to decide the best order for this series of half-hour programmes to be shown between 1 pm and 6 pm.

Fanbase Music – all the latest hits on the club scene.

Toddlestop – find out what's happening at the playgroup today!

The Street Detectives – local youth club members solve a mystery.

Sparky Art – fun arts and crafts that primary school age children can do at home.

Children's News – daily news programme for the 7–13 age group.

School Daze – soap about life for students and teachers at Daystone Comprehensive.

Brad Reckless Superhero – wild and wacky cartoon superhero series for pre-teens.

The News – bringing adults up to date with the day's events and weather.

Rhyme Time – singing, dancing and making music for the under 5s.

The Bedtime Story – stories read aloud by celebrities to the under 6s.

Good Afternoon – Jules and Gordon host this mix of news, views, cookery, hobbies and fashion.

Step 1   Make sure that what you want to say is relevant

Before you speak, ask yourself:

● What is my group trying to achieve by having this discussion?

  e.g. We've got to come up with a list showing what order a TV channel should show its programmes between lunch and 6 pm.

● What is the person who is speaking at the moment saying?

  e.g. The toddler programmes should be on at 4 pm.

● What do I want to say?

  e.g. I think it would be better to have toddler programmes earlier – before school children come home ...

● Does what I've got to say fit in with the group's purpose and what is being said now? If it does, **go for it!**

Step 2   Taking it in turns to talk

1   In your group, spend two minutes talking about what types of people are likely to be watching television between 2 pm and 4 pm. Focus on taking it in turns to speak. You know that it's your turn when:

  ● someone uses your name to begin or end a question

  ● someone is looking at you as they pause

  ● someone moves their open hand towards you

  ● you have something useful to say and there's a pause.

2   Now spend two minutes discussing what types of people are most likely to be watching television between 4 pm and 6 pm. As you do this, make sure everyone can join in. You could try using these techniques:

  ● Giving other people the chance to talk, especially if they are hanging back or not saying very much.

  ● Looking at other people while you are speaking.

  ● Asking someone a question, beginning or ending with their name.

  ● Opening your hand(s) towards someone, to show that you want to know what they think about what you are saying.

  ● Joining in the discussion, looking the person who is speaking in the eyes, leaning forward slightly and moving your hand towards them. Speaking when they pause.

Step 3 Choosing your words carefully

1 Look at the transcript of a discussion below. The phrases in bold are very useful. Each phrase does a different job. Find and list phrases that you can use to:

- agree
- disagree
- ask a question in a straightforward way
- ask a question in a more open way
- build on what has been said
- explain your point of view.

> **Support**
>
> Look at the phrases you have listed in each group and decide which are:
> - phrases you use confidently already
> - phrases you understand and could have a go at using
> - phrases you have never heard before.

Speaker 1: *Older people will be watching TV after lunch.*

Speaker 2: **No,** *they'll be having a nap.*

Speaker 3: **Yes, I agree** *it'll be lots of toddlers and adults who don't work.*

Speaker 4: **That's true** *and* **the way I see it** *we can't have programmes that suit both those groups!*

Speaker 1: *'We can't suit everyone. How about having a couple of short toddler programmes and then something for the adults?*

Speaker 2: **What** *about doing it the other way round?* **Won't** *the toddlers be having a nap?*

Speaker 3: *OK, naps are a good point.* **I wonder whether** *elderly people will be having a nap too? My gran falls asleep after lunch.*

Speaker 4: **How do you feel about** *having the adult programme in between the toddlers' programmes?*

Speaker 1: **No,** *that's not right, it'll just be confusing.*

Speaker 2: **Well the way I see it** *we should have adult followed by toddler programmes.*

2 Add any other phrases you can think of to each list.

3 Practise using these phrases as you spend two minutes continuing the conversation in your group, this time deciding which programmes to have between 1 pm and 2.30 pm in the viewing schedule. Give yourself one point for each phrase you include and see who can get the highest score.

Reinforce your skills

TopTV wants to launch a music show that will appeal to the widest possible teenage audience.

1 Working in a group, brainstorm a list of the most important music show ingredients.

2 Discuss what the show needs to have to be popular with the largest possible number of teenagers. What is vital? What must be avoided?

3 As a group, put together a proposal for the music show using the format below. When you present your proposal to the rest of the class you need to give reasons for your choices.

> **Show name:**
>
> **Host(s):**
>
> **Programme content:**

4 After listening to each group's ideas, vote on which would work best.

Stretch

Try to use this problem-solving strategy to help your group put together a proposal:
1. Sum up the problem, e.g. We've got to think of a music show that ...
2. What outcomes do we need? e.g. A programme that appeals to different teenage groups.
3. What are the difficulties? e.g. Boring if just one video after the other, need a good host ...
4. Break each difficulty down into smaller parts, e.g. The different styles of music are ...
5. Start to think of solutions.

Extend your skills

Often when you work in a group you are using talk to solve a problem or discuss an idea. As you listen to other people's contributions, try to build on what others say by:

- **Promoting** – giving reasons why what someone said was a good idea, e.g. Yes, I agree because.

- **Opposing** – giving reasons why something someone else said was not a good idea, e.g. but what about? I disagree because ...

- **Exploring** – thinking through what others are suggesting, e.g. so would that mean that...? What effect would that have ...?

- **Questioning** – asking others to give more detail or reasons, e.g. Why do you think that?

Work in two groups to complete the tasks below, taking it in turns to be the group who discusses and the group who observes.

Group A

Your task is to come up with ideas for a new soap that will attract a teenage audience. Discuss which are the four most important ingredients a soap needs to have to attract teenage viewers. Choose from:

lots of little plots	romance
characters viewers like	relationships between children and parents
nasty characters	arguments
real-life issues	exciting endings

Try to use all of the different ways of contributing to discussions.

Group B

Each choose a member of Group A to observe. Look out for examples of this group member promoting, opposing, exploring or questioning. Give them feedback on how effectively they build on what others say.

Apply your learning

Task
TVWorld is looking for a new game show to attract a huge family audience on Saturday nights. Work in a group to discuss what the game show should be like. To do well in this task you need to make sure that:

- everyone joins in the discussion making clear and relevant contributions and respecting other members of the group

- you contribute to the discussion in different ways, building on what others say.

Use these questions to help guide your discussion:

> How will the game work? e.g. Contestants have to search for ...
>
> Who will host the game show?
>
> Who will be the contestants? e.g. celebrities, adults, teenagers, children, pairs of people ...
>
> What will be the prize?
>
> What is it about your game show that will make people want to turn on and watch it every Saturday night?

Assess to Progress

How good are you now at:

● making clear and relevant contributions to a group discussion?

● helping the discussion go well by promoting, opposing, exploring and questioning?

Look back at the original scores you gave yourself on page 25. Think carefully about how you did in the task on page 30, and write down your new scores. Then convince someone who was in your group that your scores should change.

1	2	3	4	5	6	7

I find this difficult.   I'm getting there.   I'm good at this.

Skills For Life

The School Council has been given £200 to improve the look of your school. You are taking part in a meeting of the Facilities Committee. Your task is to decide how to use the money effectively – whether to spend it on one specific area (e.g. improving a cloakroom or garden), or whether to spend it on a variety of different, smaller projects. Work in a group of four to eight.

● Explain the project and give each member of the group time to think of their own ideas.

● In the discussion, take turns to share your ideas, making relevant points about how the money could be used and expressing these ideas clearly.

● Respond to other people's ideas and use different techniques to build on what they say, e.g. giving reasons why you agreed or disagreed with them or asking questions to help explore their ideas.

● Help the discussion to succeed by coming to a final decision, e.g. 'Are there any projects which we could definitely rule out at this stage?' 'Which projects do people seem to be most positive about?'

Speaking and Listening AF5
Progress in ... Drama, role play and performance

LEARNING OBJECTIVES

- Explore ideas and issues through drama.
- Work on your own and with others to develop dramatic roles.
- Comment on the effectiveness of the different dramatic techniques you use.

Activate your learning

Working with a partner, imagine that one of you is a parent and the other is their child. The parent has to tell the child that because he or she has not been able to get enough work, they cannot afford to spend any money on Christmas presents this year. The child had set their heart on a new MP3 player. Act out a short scene where the parent breaks the news.

Assess to Progress

How well can you act, role-play and perform? Rate yourself for each skill by deciding which number on the scale below shows your level best.

1	2	3	4	5	6	7

I find this difficult.   I'm getting there.   I'm good at this.

- I can work on my own and with others to create effective characters and develop dramatic performances.

  Self-check: I can choose the right kind of voice, gesture and movement to create a character and act out playscripts or improvise performances.

- I can use drama and role play to help me explore different texts and other ideas and issues.

  Self-check: When I am reading a novel, I can use hot-seating to help me understand character better.

- I can give feedback to others on their performances and respond to feedback on my own performance.

  Self-check: I know how to give advice effectively, commenting on what someone does well in performance as well as things to improve.

Build your skills

The way a character speaks can help an audience to understand how they are feeling. Read the script below. It is the opening scene of a play called *Two Weeks with the Queen* and shows an Australian family watching the Queen's speech on Christmas Day.

QUEEN	And a very merry Christmas to you all.
COLIN	Merry flamin' Christmas. (LUKE *strafes him.*) Gerroff!
LUKE	Wanna go?
COLIN	Get lost.

> LUKE *does a circle of the room shooting down the enemy and swoops on* COLIN *again.* COLIN *throws a shoe at him.*

LUKE	He hit me! Dad, he hit me!
DAD	Don't hit your brother, Colin.
COLIN	I didn't…
MUM	You heard your father.
COLIN	It was him, he started…
DAD	That's enough! We're trying to listen to the Queen here.
COLIN	Nobody ever listens to me.
LUKE	That's cos you're not the Queen.
DAD	Just keep it down to a roar, eh?

1 If you were directing this play, what advice would you give to the actors playing Colin and Luke about how they should say each of their lines? Think about how the way they speak could show how the characters are feeling. Discuss your ideas with a partner. Create a table like the one below to record your ideas.

Lines	How to say them	Why
Colin – Gerroff!	Snarling	

Reinforce your skills

Hot-seating is a technique you can use to help you get to know the character you are playing. When you are in the hot seat, other people ask you questions about your character (such as what you are thinking or how you are feeling) and you answer them in role.

1   Working with a partner, act out this extract from the play. Here, Colin is flying to England to stay with relatives whilst his brother Luke is in hospital being treated for cancer. A businessman is sitting next to Colin on the plane and they have just eaten their in-flight meal.

COLIN	(*to the* BUSINESSMAN) Lifejackets! Great. You think we better get ours out? You'd be right. In the water, I mean. Got enough fat on you to keep you warm. I'd be a gonner. (*The noise rises in pitch.*) Woa, some speed eh? Did you know most plane crashes happen on take-off? (*They lean back as the plane takes off.*) Hey, there's Sydney harbour bridge. Isn't it beautiful? My brother's in Sydney, in hospital. You reckon they're all lookin' up at us while we're lookin' down? I bet him and all the Nurses are lookin' out the hospital window at us. Wave, go on, just in case. I bet he's ropable, he only got to go in the air ambulance, I'm in a jumbo. Boo sucks Lukey mate!
	Later.
	Gor, they don't half feed you a lot. I'm as stuffed as a Christmas turkey.
	The BUSINESSMAN *gives a grunt of pain.*
	Is that a bit of cancer?
BUSINESSMAN	I beg your pardon?
COLIN	Cancer. It's where the cells start growing too fast inside your body and your whole system can go bung. I've been reading up on it.
BUSINESSMAN	I know what it is. I just don't particularly want to talk about it.
COLIN	Funny that. My folks are the same. Why not?
BUSINESSMAN	Because it's not a very pleasant topic.
COLIN	There's worse topics. (*He thinks.*) Like nuclear war and why sick has carrots in it. (*The* BUSINESSMAN *groans.*) Only, if you've got it, I'd have it seen to.
BUSINESSMAN	I haven't got it! I've got indigestion.
COLIN	Mum always gets indigestion if she bolts her tucker.

2   Now take turns to hot-seat each character and ask them questions about what they were thinking and feeling during this scene.

Support

Try and draw on your own feelings to help put yourself into the mind of the character you are playing. Think about how the businessman might feel about sitting next to a young boy who won't shut up. If you are acting out Colin's role, think about how you might feel if a member of your family was suffering from a serious illness and you were sent away from home.

3 Using what you now know about the two characters, act out the scene again. What changes did you make?

Extend your skills

As well as the way you speak, your body language is also important. The way you move, the gestures you use and your facial expressions can all help to create a believable character and an effective performance.

1 Think back to the scene on page 34 that you acted out. Discuss with your partner what body language each character could have used to show their mood and emotions.

Support

To help you think about how moods can be expressed through gestures, match the following moods and gestures.

Emotion	Gestures
Anger	Eyes wide open. Hands held out in front of you. Mouth open.
Happiness	Arms gripped around your chest. Head moving quickly from side to side.
Surprise	Big smile. Lots of movement with the arms.
Fear	Snarl. Eyes narrow. Fists gripped.

2 a) Working with your partner, act out the scene on page 34, but this time don't speak any of the lines, just use your body language (gestures, movements, expressions) to express the emotions the characters are feeling. Ask another pair to watch and give you feedback on your performance. They should think about:

- how easy it is to tell what is happening without the dialogue

- whether the body language used matches the emotions the actors are trying to express

- whether any of the body language could be changed or exaggerated to increase its impact.

b) Watch the other pair act out the same scene. What did you notice about the way they used body language to show emotion? What advice would you give them?

3 Act out the scene again, this time speaking the lines as well. Think about the way you can use your voice as well as your body language to show the character's mood. Ask the other pair to watch and give you feedback on your performance. They should:

- pick out techniques that work well, such as emphasising a particular word, and explain why these were effective

- describe any parts of the performance that aren't as effective and suggest ways to improve these

- demonstrate particular techniques that you could use to improve your performance.

Stretch

Working in your pair, improvise how the scene between Colin and the businessman continues. Think about how you can use voice, gesture and movement to sustain the character you have created.

Apply your learning

Task Whilst Colin is in England, his parents stay in Australia to look after his brother Luke who is in hospital being treated for cancer. Working in a group of three, improvise a scene involving Luke and his parents. You should use the skills you have practised in the unit to create believable characters and develop an effective dramatic performance.

Before you start your improvisation, discuss the following questions:

- Where are you going to set the scene?

- What mood do you want to create in the scene?

- How will you create the character of Luke and show what he's thinking and feeling?

- How will you create the characters of Luke's parents and show their emotions?

Assess to Progress

Think about the different roles you have created and the scenes you have performed in this unit. How do you think you have developed your skills in drama, role play and performance? Answer the following questions to help you to think about the progress you have made:

- How confident would you be at using hot-seating to explore what a character in a play or novel is thinking or feeling?

- How effectively do you think you could show a character's different emotions, through your use of voice, gesture and movement?

- How well do you think you give feedback to others on their dramatic performances? How do you respond to the feedback you get on your own performance?

Discuss your answers with a partner and think about which areas you need to improve.

1	2	3	4	5	6	7

I find this difficult.   I'm getting there.   I'm good at this.

Skills for Life

You are preparing for a work experience placement. The aim is to see how you might deal with customers in a shop. You are asked to imagine that you work in a jeweller's shop. A customer comes in, clearly in a hurry, to collect a watch that they left for repair. The person who was repairing it is on his lunch break and has gone into town, so you aren't sure whether it has been repaired or where it is. The customer is getting increasingly irritated and impatient. You should:

- stay calm as the assistant but impatient as the customer

- use formal language as the assistant, e.g. 'sorry madam'

- try to suggest how you might help the customer, e.g. 'Could I give you a call as soon as my colleague returns from lunch?'

LEARNING OBJECTIVES ⭐

- Identify some of the ways in which spoken English varies depending on place and situation.
- Understand about dialect and spoken standard English.
- Change the way that you speak for different situations.

Activate your learning

Have you ever been told to speak properly? When people use the term 'speaking properly' they often mean that they want you to use standard English. This doesn't mean that other types of spoken English are wrong, but these are called non-standard English **dialects**. A dialect is a way of speaking (the vocabulary and grammar used). A non-standard dialect might be special to a particular part of the country or a group of people. This is different from **accent** which is the way a person pronounces words.

The poem on the opposite page is by the Scottish poet, Liz Lochhead, and describes her first day at school. The first and third sections are written in a Scottish dialect, but the second and fourth are written in standard English.

1. Working with a partner, read the poem out loud. How did you find listening to the poem read out loud?

2. Make a list of all the dialect words and phrases you can find in the first verse of the poem. Next to each one, write down the standard English words or phrases used in the second verse of the poem that have the same meaning. For example:

   wis = was   gey driech = really dismal

3. In this poem, Liz Lochhead describes how she was taught to use standard English rather than her own dialect when she started school. How do you think she feels about this? Discuss your ideas with a partner.

Kidspoem/Bairnsang

it wis January
and a gey driech day
the first day Ah went to the school
so my Mum happed me up in ma
good navy-blue napp coat wi the rid tartan hood
birled a scarf aroon ma neck
pu'ed oan ma pixie an' my pawkies
it wis that bitter
said noo ye'll no starve
gie'd me a wee kiss and a kid-oan skelp oan the bum
and sent me aff across the playground
tae the place A'd learn to say

it was January
and a really dismal day
the first day I went to school
so my mother wrapped me up in my
best navy-blue top coat with the red tartan hood,
twirled a scarf around my neck,
pulled on my bobble-hat and mittens
it was so bitterly cold
said now you won't freeze to death
gave me a little kiss and a pretend slap on the bottom
and sent me off across the playground
to the place I'd learn to forget to say

it wis January
and a gey driech day
the first day Ah went to the school
so my Mum happed me up in ma
good navy-blue napp coat wi the rid tartan hood,
birled a scarf aroon ma neck,
pu'ed oan ma pixie and' ma pawkies
it wis that bitter.

Oh saying it was one thing
But when it came to writing it
In black and white
The way it had to be said
Was as if you were posh, grown-up, male, English and dead.

Assess to Progress

How good are you already at using spoken language in a way that suits the situation and audience? How good are you at noticing how others speak? Discuss the following questions with a partner. For each one place yourself on the scale below.

1	2	3	4	5	6	7

I find this difficult.   I'm getting there.   I'm good at this.

- How good are you at spotting different kinds of spoken language?

  Self-check: Can you tell the difference between standard English and non-standard dialects?

- How good are you at deciding when it is best to use standard English and when it is best to use your own dialect?

  Self-check: Which would you use when speaking to a friend at break time? Which would you use if you were speaking to a visitor to your school?

- How good are you at commenting on the effects of different kinds of spoken English?

  Self-check: In different situations, are you able to say when speakers have made good choices about the words that they have used?

Build your skills

1 Look at the speaking situations listed below. For each one, decide whether you would expect the speaker or speakers to use standard English or whether they would be more likely to speak informally, using non-standard English.

a) A head teacher talking to pupils in assembly

b) Two pupils chatting at break time about last night's TV

c) A news reporter on television

d) A presenter of a teenage music programme interviewing a band

2 a) Place each of the situations on the following scale.

1   2   3   4   5   6   7

Informal   Formal

        b) Explain to a partner why you have placed each situation where they are on the scale. Discuss what this scale shows you about different levels of formality.

How can you tell the difference between standard English and non-standard English? The **vocabulary** used in non-standard English can include dialect words and phrases, such as 'Where's he to?' (a dialect phrase from Bristol meaning 'Where's that?') and slang such as 'props' (which means 'respect'). However, spoken non-standard English can also use different **grammar** (the way words are put together in a sentence), for example using negatives such as 'I ain't' instead of 'I am not', subject–verb agreements such as 'they was' instead of 'they were' and demonstrative pronouns, such as 'them books' instead of 'those books'.

3 a) Look at the following pairs of sentences. For each one, decide which sentence uses standard English and which one uses non-standard English.

Me and Sam are going to the cinema.	Sam and I are going to the cinema.
I don't want any.	I don't want none.
They was hanging around outside.	They were hanging around outside.
I ain't listening to you no more.	I am not listening you any more.
Chelsea should of won that match.	Chelsea should have won that match.

        b) Discuss your choices with a partner and talk about how you made your decisions. Are there any sentences where you disagreed?

Reinforce your skills

Choosing whether to use standard English or your own dialect can depend on your relationship to the person you are speaking to or the situation.

In the example below the manager of a music store is interviewing three teenagers for a sales job. Read their responses to his questions.

Mike

Jo

Hasan

Manager: How did you find out about this job?

Hasan: I saw the ad in the paper.

Jo: I saw the advertisement in the local newspaper.

Mike: I could of seen it in the local rag.

Manager: Why do you want this job?

Jo: I think I offer the right skills to be really successful in this role.

Hasan: I think it'd be really cool to work here.

Mike: I'd be bang on at this job, don't you reckon?

Manager: Is there anything that would prevent you from getting to work on time?

Mike: No way mate, I ain't no slacker.

Jo: If the bus arrives on time, I should always be in work early.

Hasan: I sometimes oversleep, but I'm getting myself a new alarm clock.

1 Working with in pairs, decide who you think would get the job and why. Discuss how much you were influenced by **what** they said and how much by **how** they said it.

2 Discuss how you would answer the questions.

3 Working in groups, role-play the rest of the interview. Before you begin:

   ● brainstorm the interview questions that could be asked

   ● decide who should play the manager and how they should speak

- think about what type of language each interviewee would use, e.g. Would Mike continue to use slang in his answers?

Extend your skills

The language choices you make when you speak don't just depend on the situation you are in. Where you come from also makes a difference. Look at this map of the UK which shows some dialect words and phrases used by people in different parts of the country.

1 Working with a partner, discuss how many of the dialect words listed you have heard before and give examples of times you have heard these.

2 Find where you live on the map. Which dialect words and phrases do you use? Add them to the map. Be ready to explain what each one means.

Gie's a schifter: let me have a go/look

Canny: something or someone good

Happen or 'appen: perhaps

Spondoolicks: money

Mardy: moody

Her's in a cank!: she is in a bad mood

Noggorhead: idiot

Edinburgh

Tyneside

Yorkshire

Liverpool

Mid-Wales

Black country

Somerset

Support

Think about the words that you use for:
- attractive or unattractive
- having lots of money or being poor.

Stretch

Some words that start out as dialect words from one part of the country or community can become widespread. For example, 'nang' meaning 'cool' and 'diss' meaning 'insult' are words that started out in in the Jamaican community in London, but are now widely known. Can you think of any other examples? How could you find out whether the dialect words on your list originally come from your local area or from else where?

Apply your learning

Task Working with a partner, you are going to carry out an investigation into the way spoken English is used in your local area.

1   Using the list of dialect words you created in the previous section, interview friends, members of your family or teachers to find out:

   ● which of the dialect words they know the meaning of

   ● which of the dialect words they use in their own speech and when they use these

   ● any other local dialect words they know and what meanings these have.

You should interview at least three different people to help you to get a range of answers. Keep a note of who you have interviewed.

2   Use the information you have found out to prepare a short presentation to the rest of the class about the dialect that people in your local area use. In your presentation, you should comment on:

   ● which dialect words are most commonly used in your area. Remember to explain what these mean using standard English

   ● when dialect words and phrases are usually used, giving examples that you have found out from your investigation

   ● whether there were any differences in the dialect words used by different people

   ● how you feel about your local dialect.

3   At the end of your presentations, be ready to answer questions from the rest of the class. For example, you might be asked to explain any differences you found between the dialect words used by younger and older people.

Assess to Progress

How good are you now at using spoken language in a way that suits the setting and audience? How good are you at noticing how others speak?

1 Think about the activities you have completed in this unit and answer the questions below. For each question, rate yourself on the scale below.

1	2	3	4	5	6	7

I find this difficult.   I'm getting there.   I'm good at this.

- How good are you at deciding when it is best to use standard English?

- How good are you at adapting your language appropriately for different situations?

- How good are you at spotting different kinds of spoken language?

- How good are you at commenting on the effects of different kinds of spoken English?

2 Discuss with a partner what you need to do to improve the skills you have worked on in this unit further.

SKILLs FOR LIFE

You are sometimes asked to give tours of the school to visitors and potential new pupils. Working with a partner, think about how you would speak and listen if you were asked to show around the Chair of Governors so that she can see the school in action. The Chair of Governors is a businesswoman who runs a large financial company.

Then think about how you might show around a Year 7 student who has just moved from a much smaller school and is feeling nervous about the change.

With your partner, role-play what the start of each tour might sound like:

- Plan how you would introduce yourself, what you would say about the school to introduce it, and how you might start the tour.

- Talk about how you might approach each tour differently – the words and phrases you will use.

- Ask for feedback from your partner on how you use language differently in each task.

Speaking and Listening
Assessing your Progress

- Develop some of your ideas and feelings when you talk to others.
- Use your voice to help your listeners follow the important points you are making.
- Make sensible contributions and respect other members of the group.
- Be able to move from formal to informal use of language.
- Improvise a conversation in role, using voice, gesture and movement.

Working through this unit will give you the opportunity to show the progress you have made in your speaking and listening skills. You will explore how good speakers express themselves, try out some ideas and complete three tasks, where you will have the chance to show your skills in talking to others, with others, and in drama.

Activate your learning

1   What do you think are the most important ingredients for good speaking and listening? Make a list of as many ideas as you can.

Support
Think of the people who speak to you in school, e.g. pupils at break time, teachers in lessons or corridors, Head of Year in assembly. In what different ways do they use their voice and body to make their point and get your attention? How do people show they are listening to them?

2   Take one of your ideas and with a partner work out an explanation of how to do it well.

Stretch
With a partner, use your explanation of how to speak or listen well to plan a demonstration that shows:
- what it is like when it is done badly. Think about the sorts of mistakes people often make and include those.
- what it is like when it is done well.
Be prepared to show your ideas to your class.

Progress task 1: Talking to others

You have won a radio competition to be guest of honour at a live music event in your local area. As part of the prize you will need to tell radio listeners about your experiences that day.

You will have three minutes to give an account of the most memorable part of your day. Your listeners will want to know what it was like to meet the musicians, be treated as a VIP and listen to the live performances.

Assess to Progress

In this task you will be assessed on the way you:

- develop some of your ideas and feelings
- use your voice for expression
- begin to use sentences that are different lengths and structures
- decide how formal your language should be.

1   Look at the examples of people at Radio 1 talking about the radio station. Listen very carefully and note:

- which words they emphasise
- how they use their hands and faces to support what they are saying
- how they use pauses to change the pace of what they are saying.

2   Think of a time when you have told a story or explained an event to someone. Which of the following key skills did you use when you were speaking? Pick out three skills that you think you are good at and make a note of these. Pick out three skills that you think you need to improve and discuss with a partner how you will develop these skills.

Look for the reactions of my listeners and adapt what I say	Know when to use standard English	Try not to hesitate or use too many 'filler words' that will distract the listener, e.g. 'um', 'er', 'right', 'so'
Have a shape for what I want to say. Don't just keep adding points with 'and'	Vary the speed I am talking at	Vary the length and structure of my sentences
Make eye contact with the person I am speaking to	Vary the volume I am speaking at	Use body language to help express my feelings
Use expression in my voice to show feelings	Choose words that will make what I say interesting	Show the speaker that I am listening and understand

Before you start to prepare your account of the day out at a music event, look at the two accounts of other days out below.

3 a) Look at this account describing a fantastic day at a fun park. With a partner, practise saying it so that you:

- emphasise key words,
- speed up and slow down to make it sound exciting,
- use gestures to help you show your feelings.

Our day out was absolutely fantastic. We really did have a brilliant time – it was incredible. The weather was gorgeous for the whole day, the food was delicious and the rides were awesome! The best one was the Spin Dipper which is a new ride involving pods which spin round and round and dip up and down all at the same time. It was heart-stopping. But we all really enjoyed it and rushed to join to queue to have another go!

b) Now count all the different ways the speaker describes having a good time.

c) Which is the longest sentence in this account? Which is the shortest? Why do you think they have been organised like that?

d) Which words and phrases do you think are the most formal and the most informal?

4 Look at this account describing a fantastic day at an aquapark.

a) With a partner, practise saying it so that you:

- emphasise key words
- speed up and slow down to make it sound exciting
- use gestures to help you show your feelings.

We had a fab time at the aquapark. It was a great day. There was loads of stuff to do. There was a wave machine and some big slides. The best one went from the top of the building and into two splash pools and another chute then it ended up in a heated outdoor pool. There was a water sports area and we played water volleyball. There was a café for refreshments which was great. We had a laugh.

b) How could you improve it?

- What different words could the speaker use to describe how exciting the experience was?

- What do you notice about the length of the sentences? Which would you change?

- Which words are informal and which are formal? Do you think these have been used in the best way?
  How would you change it?

5 When talking to others it can be helpful to plan what you are going to say. Look back at the task on page 47. Plan your account of your time at the live music event:

- Which part of the event are you going to focus on?
  You will need to make some notes of the key points.

- Remember to include your feelings as well as what happened.

- Decide how you are going to start and end your account. What information does the listener need at the start? How will you round off the information to show you have finished?

- Which words could you use to make what you say interesting to the listeners?

- Remember that you have only got three minutes!

6 Working in groups, take turns to give your account. Before you start remind yourself of the task. You may use your notes if you need to. When you are listening to other people, help them by showing you are interested.

7 When you have completed your talk, look again at the skills box on page 47. Which of these skills did you use? Make a note of these and think how about you could use the others next time.

Progress task 2: Talking with others

You are now going to show how effectively you can talk to others when you work in a small group. This means you will need to:

- listen and respond

- make sensible contributions in a group discussion

You are going to be discussing the following topic:

Do you think Radio 1 appeals to teenage listeners? How could it improve its appeal to this audience? You should discuss:

- the range of music it plays

- the DJs it employs

- other things that Radio 1 does, such as organising live music events

- what you like and dislike about the station.

First, you need to remind yourself about good discussion skills.

1 a) Working in a group of four, discuss what skills you need to use to have a good group discussion. Create a list of five key points to remember. You should include points about listening as well as speaking.

b) As you discuss, think about the speaking and listening skills you are using and try to put the points you discuss into action. You could chose a chairperson to lead the discussion and make sure that everybody has a chance to contribute their ideas. You should also chose a spokesperson to share your list of points with the rest of the class.

Assess to Progress

In this task you will be assessed on the way you:

- show that you are listening to others and understanding the main points they are making

- make sensible contributions and respect other members of the group

- vary the tone of your voice to express your feelings

- use talk to help you think through your ideas more clearly.

Now think about the discussion task you are going to complete.

2   On your own, spend one minute thinking about what you know about Radio 1. Note down the points you want to make in the discussion. You could use a spider diagram or a list to make your notes, for example:

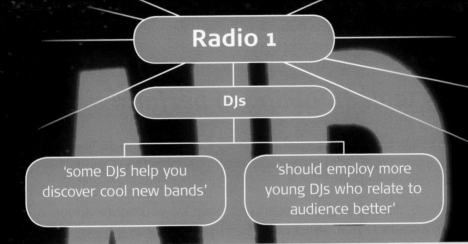

Stretch

Think about other viewpoints as well as your own. For example:
- Teenagers have different interests and backgrounds, and range in age from 13 to 19-years-old. How does this affect what would appeal to them?
- What do you think Radio 1's viewpoint is?
- Radio 1 is a national radio station controlled by the BBC. How might this affect what they can do to appeal to young people?
- What impact might the costs involved have on what they can do?

3   Now think about the speaking and listening skills you are going to use in this task. Try to answer these questions:

- How can you make sure you present the points you want to make in a way that will encourage other people to listen to you?

- How will you show you are listening to other people's views?

- What will you do if someone else mentions a point that you were going to make?

- How will you contribute to the discussion?

Support

Look back at the box on page 47. What are the five different ways that you can use to add your ideas to a discussion?

4   Now work as a group to complete the task. Discuss whether Radio 1 appeals to teenage listeners and agree on ways you think the station could improve its appeal to this audience.

5   When you have completed your discussion, review the skills you used. Look at the success criteria opposite and decide how you would rate yourself for each skill. Make a note of what you did well and how you could improve next time.

Progress task 3: Talking to perform

Radio 1 is keen to use lots of regional voices so that it appeals to listeners all over the country. Local radio stations also employ presenters who represent the local community.

1   Listen to these clips of Radio 1 presenters. What do you notice about the way they speak? What effect does hearing these voices have on you? Is it just their accent that is different or something else about the way they speak?

Stretch

What is the effect of the way the presenter speaks in this tour? What do you notice about the camera movement and shots? What is the effect?

You are going to complete a task that involves talking to perform.

You, and several other listeners, have received an invitation from your local radio station to attend an open day. It is a chance to meet the DJs and have a tour of the building. You will choose a character to play and improvise a short conversation with other guests.

Assess to Progress

In this task you will be assessed on the way you:

- improvise a dramatic situation
- develop characters through using voice, gesture and movement
- choose the right words to develop your character.

2 a) You need to decide who you are going to be in this role play. Here are some ideas:

- a fan of a particular type of music or radio show
- a parent of teenage children who wants to keep up to date with local events
- a youth worker who likes to know about the latest music
- a tradesman who listens to the radio through an MP3 player while working
- an elderly person who listens to the radio for company during the day.

b) Decide what sort of personality you want to have. Decide how you feel about going to the open day: are you excited? Or curious? Have you visited a radio station before?

c) Think about how you can use your voice, gestures and movement to show other people what you are like.

3 Working with a partner, think about the character you will play and discuss how you could make the way you act and speak show the character you are. Practise introducing yourself to each other. Would your character speak formally, using standard English, or would they be more likely to speak informally to you, perhaps using a regional dialect?

4 You are now going to complete the task. Reread the information to remind yourself of the situation. Imagine you have arrived at the open day. You are asked to wait for the tour to start. You stand in two circles, one inside the other.

a) Face a partner and improvise a short conversation with them. You could talk about who you are, what you are looking forward to in the tour, the music you enjoy and what you think about the radio station.

b) After one minute, you will move to your left and will meet a new partner. Have another conversation with them, remembering to act in role through your voice, gestures and movement.

c) You might be able to speak to several different characters. Try to develop your role each time you speak to a new person.

d) When you have finished the activity, make a note in your speaking and listening diary of the different ways you used your voice, gestures and movement to show your character.

Stretch

Join up with the partners you spoke to in the task. Compare your speaking and listening diaries and discuss how each of you changed the way you spoke to create your character.

Assess to Progress

You have completed three tasks: talking to others, talking with others and talking to perform.

Decide what skills you have used and the progress you have made.

Rate yourself for each skill by deciding which number on the scale below shows your skill level best.

1	2	3	4	5	6	7

I find this difficult.　　　　I'm getting there.　　　　I'm good at this.

- When talking to others, I can develop some of my ideas and feelings.

- When talking to others and with others, I can use my voice to help my listeners follow the important points I am making.

- When talking with others, I make sensible contributions and respect other members of the group.

- When talking with others and in improvised drama, I can move from formal to informal use of language.

- When improvising a conversation in role I can use voice, gesture and movement to show my character.

Progress in ...
Reading

Progress in ... Reading and responding to different texts

LEARNING OBJECTIVES

- Use a range of reading strategies to read different texts in different ways.
- Learn which are the best reading strategies to use to understand and enjoy new texts.

Activate your learning

Below are four extracts from texts. There are no visual clues to help you to know what they are.

1 Quickly read each extract and think about what kind of text it may be from, for example, a novel or a recipe.

A
My arrival at infant school was one of the most spectacular experiences of my young life. I had no sooner walked in through the elaborate wrought-iron gates (why do all schools have elaborate gates, forever open, forever useless, except for climbing on?) than I was met from one side by a hail of half-bricks and from the other by a charging mob of young gods with lavatory brush hair.

B
The best treatment for mouth ulcers. Gargle with salt water. You should find that it works a treat. Salt is cheap and easy to get hold of and we all have it at home, so no need to splash out and spend lots of money on expensive mouth ulcer creams.

C
'Come on, big man. Chase that ball. Boot it up the field. He's on your back. Aaaah!!! What you playing at?'

Jimmy's head went down. But that didn't matter. He could see what GI Joe was doing without looking.

D
Wash the nettles well, drain, put them into plenty of water with a little salt, boil for twenty minutes, or a little longer.

2   Now answer these questions to explore each text a bit more.

Which text ...	A, B, C or D?	How can you tell? Write down one word or phrase that helps you decide.
a) is most factual?		
b) feels most like a made-up story?		
c) seems most modern?		
d) contains the word 'boil'?		
e) consists of four sentences?		

3   Finally, think about how you approached this two-part reading task.

a) Part 1 asked you to read the texts quickly. Talk to a partner about how you approached the task of reading short texts quickly.

b) Part 2 asked you to make judgements and find specific information.

- How did you decide which were the most factual and most modern texts and which was a made-up story?

- How did you find the word 'boil'?

- What did you do to find the text with four sentences?

- Which of the questions in part 2 did you find easiest to answer? Why?

Assess to Progress

How well can you pick out and comment on information from texts already?

Rate yourself for each skill by deciding which number on the scale below shows your skill level best.

| 1 | 2 | 3 | 4 | 5 | 6 | 7 |

I find this difficult.   I'm getting there.   I'm good at this.

- I can read different texts in different ways.

  Self-check: You read a story carefully, from beginning to end, but you read a web page by scanning for the interesting or useful bits.

- I can get the overall message of a text from reading it quickly.

  Self-check: You're under pressure to understand some instructions. People are waiting for you. Can you cope?

- I read some texts purely for pleasure.

  Self-check: Do you still make some time simply to sit and enjoy a book or magazine?

Build your skills

In the Activate your learning activity you used the reading strategies **skimming** (reading a text quickly to get the overall meaning) and **scanning** (reading to find specific information). You can practise these strategies further in the next unit. Now you are going to build your reading skills by developing the strategies of **making predictions** and **close reading**.

Step 1   Before you start reading, make predictions

One way to improve your understanding of a text is by making some predictions about what the text will be like before you read it.

1   Think about these questions:

- You are going to read a text about 'climate change'. What do you understand by this term?

- What do you expect to learn about from the text, e.g. Will it be personal, funny, lively, scientific, technical, interesting?

- This is a non-fiction information text. What kind of vocabulary do you expect, e.g. technical, informal, unfamiliar, complicated?

- You will be asked some questions about details in the text. How do you expect to read it, e.g. slowly, making notes, skimming?

2   Make some predictions about what you expect the text to be like. Write a sentence starting like this:

> *Before reading this text, I predict …*

Step 2   Read the text closely

1   Read this paragraph about climate change. Your task is to find out what the term 'climate change' means.

WHAT IS CLIMATE CHANGE?

The climate of the Earth is always changing. In the past it has altered as a result of natural causes. Nowadays, however, the term climate change is generally used when referring to changes in our climate which have been identified since the early part of the 1900s. The changes we've seen over recent years and those which are predicted over the next 80 years are thought to be mainly as a result of human behaviour rather than due to natural changes in the atmosphere.

2 Sarah was given the task of finding out what 'climate change' means using this text. Read what she says about how she approached this task.

> 1 I **scanned** the sub-headings in this chapter to find the paragraph that contains the information I need. I'll **close read** this paragraph.

> 2 I **reread** the long sentences a few times to make sure I understood them. I **predict** that if I read on I'll find out more about these changes.

> 3 I have learnt what the term climate change means. **Questions** I now want to ask the text are: How has the climate changed in recent years? What specific things have humans done to cause these changes?

Step 3 After reading, think about what you have read

Use these questions to see how well you understand the text.

Exploring the facts

1 Write down one fact from the text.

2 Why did the Earth's climate change in the past?

3 What does the phrase 'climate change' usually refer to these days?

4 What has probably caused the main changes in the climate over the past 80 years?

Exploring the style

5 The author says 'The changes ... are thought to be mainly as a result of human behaviour rather than due to natural changes in the atmosphere.' Imagine she said 'are' instead of 'are thought to be'. How would the meaning of the text be different?

Reflecting on your performance

6 Questions 1 to 4 above are basic comprehension questions. Did you find it straightforward to find the answers?

7 Question 5 asks for an opinion. Did you find this question harder?

8 Talk to a partner about how you approached answering questions 1 to 5.

Reinforce your skills

Presentation

Reading means understanding more than just words. In many texts there are other clues too: pictures, colours, layout and graphic design that also help us to understand a message. Another reading strategy you can use is to **comment on design and layout.**

Look at this extract from a comic book version of Shakespeare's play, *As You Like It*. This was designed to help younger readers understand the story.

1   Look at the style of the pictures. Which of these words do you think best describes the overall design? Discuss your response with a partner.

> **COLOURFUL**   old-fashioned   **FUNNY**   serious   quirky   DETAILED   **disturbing**

2   Look at the first frame and read the text underneath it. In the picture, find the three characters who are mentioned in the text. Which one looks most like the way you would have drawn her or him? Explain why.

Language

Now you are going to build your understanding of this text by using another strategy: looking at the **writer's use of language**.

3   What is the main difference between the words written underneath each image and the words contained in the frame with the drawings? How is the language different and why?

4   Look at the text underneath the first image. Think of a synonym (a word or phrase with a similar meaning) that the writer could have used for each of these words:
a) fearsome
b) pining
c) banished.

5   Choose one frame and write a paragraph saying how well you think the use of pictures with words helps you to understand the story. In your response you might use words and phrases like this:

● I think that the way the character is presented seems ...

● I like the way ...

● I'm not so impressed by ...

● The use of colour is ...

● The style of the illustration seems ...

● The drawing matches the written text because ...

6   Now think about how you approached this task of reading the images alongside the words. Discuss these questions with a partner:

a) Which of the questions did you find the most difficult to answer?

b) Was responding to the details of the pictures harder than understanding the words?

c) What different reading strategies did you use, e.g. skimming, scanning, close reading?

Stretch

Imagine you have been asked to present *As You Like It* in a different style. The story contains lots of menace – fights, giants, aggression – and is set in a dark forest. Take one of the current frames and, using the same text, design a very different illustration with a darker, more disturbing feel. Underneath your drawing, write a paragraph explaining the decisions you made – what you read in the words and how you tried to present this in the image.

Extend your skills

The extract below is from the novel *Not the End of the World* by Geraldine McCaughrean. The novel tells the story of the biblical flood and life on the Ark from the point of view of Noah's daughter, Timna. This extract describes the coming of the rain.

1   Write down some **predictions** about the extract based on the information in the paragraph above. For example how will it be different from a newspaper or eyewitness account of a major flood?

2   **Skim** the text and write two sentences to summarise what happens.

It took more than rain you see. Floods, flooding: the world's seen that time past number. Every year since I was born the seasonal floods have been getting worse – uprooting whole tribes, washing away encampments, changing the course of rivers. But not all the rain under the Earth and above the sky could have done this. Somewhere over the horizon God must have pressed the flood between his hands – compressed the floodwater into a single pleat of water three mountains high and sent it hurtling across the face of the Earth faster than horses can gallop or birds fly. We looked out and saw it coming: a wall of water that blocked out the setting moon. We thought it was a field away, but it was more like fifty miles, because it just kept getting bigger and bigger … People began to run. Within twenty strides they stopped, knowing that there was nowhere to run for, no 'higher ground' high enough to save them. You could see their legs melt with terror, and they went down on their hands and knees, reaching out for anyone nearby, clasping their hands at the sky.

The air turned icy cold. Then there was no air: the Wave had breathed it all in.

3   **Scan** the text:
   a) Write down how many times the writer uses the word 'Earth'.
   b) Which word describes precisely what God does with the floodwater in his hands?
   c) The narrator says the wall of water looked as if it was just 'a field away'. How far away in miles was it?

4   Think about the **writer's use of language**:

a) The writer uses the pronouns 'we' and 'you' a lot. Describe what impression you get of the person telling the story and who she is talking to.

b) The writer uses a number of powerful visual descriptions. Use your own words or draw a sketch with arrows and labels to say what you think each of these phrases from the extract means:

- a single pleat of water three mountains high

- a wall of water that blocked out the setting moon

- you could see their legs melt with terror

- the Wave had breathed it all in.

5   Based on the extract, what do you **predict** will happen next?

6   a) If you were asked to present this extract from the story in the form of a comic book, how would you organise it? How many frames would you use? Which words would you put underneath each illustration?

b) Create one frame based on any part of the extract and quickly design it. Don't worry about your drawing skills. Instead you can use arrows and labels to explain what you are trying to create.

Support

Think about the mood of the illustrations – how will you capture the sense of danger and panic? What should the background colours be like? What should the expressions on faces be like?

Use the reading strategies you have practised so far in this unit to help you, e.g. **close reading** and **making predictions.**

Stretch

Based on your understanding of this extract, write the next paragraph of the story. What happens next? Show that you have noticed the **writer's use of language** by using a similar style.

Apply your learning

The text opposite is taken from the WWF website and explains why scientists are using electronic communication devices to track the movement of a number of polar bears. Complete the task below to demonstrate your skills in reading and responding to texts.

Task

1 a) This is a web page. Before reading it, **predict** what kind of features you expect it to contain that will make it different from a novel about polar bears or the autobiography of a scientist working in the Arctic.

   b) Write down three things that you would expect to learn from the text.

2 From **skimming** the text, write down three topics about tracking polar bears that the website covers.

3 a) From **scanning** the text, write down why only female polar bears can be tracked.

   b) Write down the things the tracking information allows scientists to learn about polar bears.

   c) What do scientists have to do to the polar bear in order to work out her age?

4 a) From looking at the web page generally, write down two things that you like about its **presentation** and two things that you would change.

   b) Look at the sub-headings in the text. Why do you think the last one is a question rather than a statement?

5 a) Use the text to make a list of ten facts or opinions you might include in a fact sheet for very young readers (aged from five to eight) telling them more about polar bears and why scientists track them.

      e.g. Scientists use radio collars to track polar bears' movements.

   b) Choose two of the facts you have listed and write them in a way that you think your target audience will clearly understand.
      e.g. Scientists put a special collar round polar bears' necks so they can find out where they go.

for a living planet

Polar Bear Tracker

| About WWF | How Can You Help | News & Facts | FAQ |

[_____] search

Home > About WWF > Europe > Solutions by Region > Arctic > Polar Bear Tracker

WWF-Canon Polar Bear Tracker

| Map Overview | Svalbard | |

N23731   N23881   N23479

Updates from the field

03 Sep 2007
Polar bear movements in August 2007

We have seen some interesting movement behaviour in the Svalbard polar bears we have been following since March 2007. Three of the bears have not moved too much and we have had a hard time keeping track of two of them. This is probably because they are travelling beneath cliff faces that interfere with the satellite signal. One of the bears, N23881, has spent most of the summer out on the pack ice and has travelled a considerable distance in the last 6 months.
» Read more

Collecting information to help protect polar bears

Scientists learn about polar bears by observing them in their natural habitat. Radio collars are used to track their movements.

Only female polar bears can be tracked using radio collars. Male polar bears have necks that are wider than their head so the collars simply fall off.

Help us to understand how they travel

The collar sends signals via satellite that are used to plot the bear's path. From the data collected scientists can determine when a female enters a den, when she emerges with cubs and how far she travels each day. The tracking also enables scientists to map a polar bear's range to determine whether individuals travel vast distances or remain strictly within their home range. Over time this information reveals changes and adaptations. For example, in years when there is less sea ice, it will tell us where bears go and how they adapt.

Help us monitor health

When scientists fit a bear with a radio collar, they also collect important information about its health. Its length and weight are measured, samples of blood, fat, hair, and other tissues are taken to identify any toxic contamination, and its age is estimated.

How do you figure out a bear's age?

As a bear grows, a thin layer of bone, called cementum, is deposited each year in the teeth. By examining a thin slice of tooth under a microscope and counting the layers of cementum, the polar bear's age can be estimated in much the same way that tree rings reveal the age of a forest. To do this, a small tooth, located just behind the large canine teeth and of no use to the bear, is pulled. This information is vital for monitoring the health and condition of polar bears over time.

Assess to Progress

How good are you now at reading and responding to new and unfamiliar texts? Are you confident that when you read a new text you know how to get what you want from it?

Complete a copy of the table below to show how well you can use each of these reading strategies.

Strategy	Rate your ability 1 = I am confident 2 = I feel OK at this 3 = I need to practise	I used this strategy when ...
Skimming to get the overall meaning of a text		
Scanning to find specific information		
Close reading to get all the detail		
Commenting on presentation		
Making predictions about a text		
Looking at the writer's use of language		

There are many more reading strategies you can use to help you get the most out of the texts you read. How many of these do you currently use?

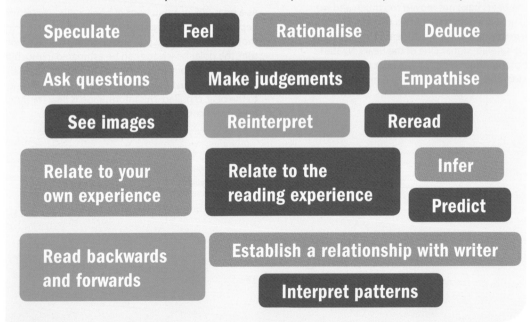

Speculate   Feel   Rationalise   Deduce

Ask questions   Make judgements   Empathise

See images   Reinterpret   Reread

Relate to your own experience   Relate to the reading experience   Infer   Predict

Read backwards and forwards   Establish a relationship with writer   Interpret patterns

You are helping children at a local primary school with their reading. The teacher there has asked the children to complete a questionnaire about their reading. Here is David's completed questionnaire:

> Do you like reading?
>
> > It's OK, but I prefer playing video games.
>
> What sort of thing do you read?
>
> > I sometimes like reading scary books by writers like Darren Shan, but mainly I read video game magazines to find out hints for the games I play.
>
> What have you read recently?
>
> > Wolf Brother by Michelle Paver
>
> Did you like it?
>
> > It was cool finding out about the stone age and some parts of the book were really frightening.
>
> What do you think you will read next?
>
> > I don't know.
>
> How do you find books to read?
>
> > If a book's got a good cover I'll give it a go.

What can you tell about the type of reader David is? Answer the following questions to help you prepare for your first reading session with David.

1 What types of book or magazine does David like to read?

2 Does David mainly read to find out information or for enjoyment? How can you tell this?

3 What was the last book David read? What did he like about it?

4 How does David choose new books to read? What advice could you give him about other ways of finding books to read?

5 What book would you give David to read next? Think about the types of book he enjoys.

6 Now answer the questionnaire yourself. What type of reader are you? Discuss your answers with a partner.

Progress in ... Developing active reading strategies

LEARNING OBJECTIVES

- Use skimming and scanning to locate the main points from print and electronic texts.
- Locate relevant information from a text.
- Make relevant notes when gathering ideas from a text.
- Make effective comments, referring to the text to support your ideas.

Activate your learning

1   Stand by for a race! The table below contains instant messaging codes used by American students. When your teacher starts the clock, see how quickly you can find the eight codes in the list below. The winner will be the person who finds all eight, giving the column and number for each one.

Here's an example to show you how:

Find: I don't know   Answer: idk – 5B

Now see how quickly you can find these codes:

a) I'll be right back   e) as a friend

b) I'm away from the computer   f) call my cellphone

c) please   g) parent emergency!

d) I have got to go   h) my parents are around

Instant messaging codes used by American students	
A	**B**
1	aaf = as a friend	afc = I'm away from the computer
2	ayt = are you there?	b4n = bye for now
3	brb = I'll be right back	cmc = call my cellphone
4	ctn = I can't talk now	cd8 or cd9 = my parents are around
5	g2g = I have got to go	idk = I don't know
6	mirl = let's meet in real life	nmu = not much, you?
7	p911 = parent emergency!	plox = please
8	ttfn = goodbye for now	tffw = too funny for words
9	ur2gr8 = you are great too	wu = what's up?

2 These three students have been asked to identify the codes that are questions. Discuss how their answers are different from each other. Which answer would be most useful for someone who:

a) does not have a copy of the table to read?

b) wants to find the questions in the table?

Zara: Three of them, for example wu = what's up?

Tom: ayt = are you there?, nmu = not much, you?, wu = what's up?

Naomi: 2A, 6B and 9B

Assess to Progress

How well can you pick out and comment on information from texts already? Rate yourself for each skill by deciding which number on the scale below shows your skill level best.

1	2	3	4	5	6	7

I find this difficult.   I'm getting there.   I'm good at this.

- I can locate the main points from texts written in different formats, e.g. charts, tables, articles, websites, stories and poems.

  Self-check: You're given a text, such as a newspaper story or website. How confidently could you pick out the five main points?

- I can pick out relevant information in a text.

  Self-check: You're writing about a novel or play. How well can you find a quotation to support your opinion?

- I can make relevant notes when using a text to gather ideas.

  Self-check: You're making a group presentation about global warming in Science. How well can you read a news article and make notes to share with the group?

- I can make effective comments on a text.

  Self-check: You've found the right quotation for your essay. How good are you at knowing what to say about it?

Build your skills

Ben is 13. He wants to buy a T-shirt online.

> I want something a bit different from everyday T-shirts, something that will grab attention when I'm out with friends. I'm happy to pay up to £20 and I'd like something eye-catching and fashionable, but not embarrassing. I'm a medium size.

Ben's search has brought up a website with the T-Qualizer on it. He needs your help to decide whether to buy it. The three skill steps below show how to search any text to find the information you need. Follow the steps to help Ben to make his decision.

Step 1 Before you start reading, work out what you need to find out

1   Why are you reading this text?

2   What key words or figures do you need to search for? Which of these sorts of word will help you to find out the information you need?

TIMES   names   **PATTERNS**   sizes   colours   ages   **prices**   fashionable

Step 2 Skim the text to get the meaning

When we **skim** read a text, we look for the overall message or gist of it. Let your eyes run quickly over the pages, picking out headings, noticing what is in pictures and where different information is placed. Then let your eyes run through the text and work out what each paragraph is about.

1   Practise **skimming** the web page opposite. What do you think are the three main features of the T-Qualizer that Ben needs to know about?

Step 3 Scan the text and make a note of the information you need

When we **scan** a text, we look for specific information. Search for key words by moving your eyes quickly over the page. You could trace your finger across lines of text to help you to spot the key words. You don't need to read every word, but you must scan the whole text.

When **making notes**, only jot down the information you need to do your task. Don't write in whole sentences. Use numbers, abbreviations and symbols instead of whole words. Make sure you'll be able to understand your notes later.

1   Scan the web page and note: a) the product ID, b) what colours the lights are, and c) what sizes are available.

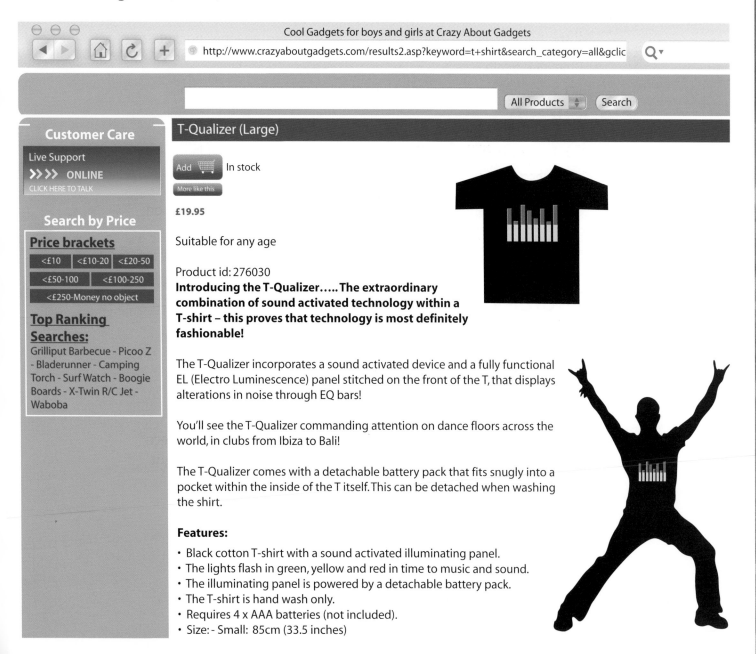

Cool Gadgets for boys and girls at Crazy About Gadgets

http://www.crazyaboutgadgets.com/results2.asp?keyword=t+shirt&search_category=all&gclic

All Products ♦   Search

Customer Care

Live Support
>> >>   ONLINE
CLICK HERE TO TALK

Search by Price

Price brackets

<£10	<£10-20	<£20-50
<£50-100		<£100-250
<£250-Money no object		

Top Ranking Searches:
Grilliput Barbecue - Picoo Z - Bladerunner - Camping Torch - Surf Watch - Boogie Boards - X-Twin R/C Jet - Waboba

T-Qualizer (Large)

Add 🛒   In stock

More like this

£19.95

Suitable for any age

Product id: 276030
Introducing the T-Qualizer….. The extraordinary combination of sound activated technology within a T-shirt – this proves that technology is most definitely fashionable!

The T-Qualizer incorporates a sound activated device and a fully functional EL (Electro Luminescence) panel stitched on the front of the T, that displays alterations in noise through EQ bars!

You'll see the T-Qualizer commanding attention on dance floors across the world, in clubs from Ibiza to Bali!

The T-Qualizer comes with a detachable battery pack that fits snugly into a pocket within the inside of the T itself. This can be detached when washing the shirt.

Features:
• Black cotton T-shirt with a sound activated illuminating panel.
• The lights flash in green, yellow and red in time to music and sound.
• The illuminating panel is powered by a detachable battery pack.
• The T-shirt is hand wash only.
• Requires 4 x AAA batteries (not included).
• Size: - Small: 85cm (33.5 inches)

Step 4   Look at the relevance of information

Remind yourself why you need the information you are looking for. Look at the information you have found and ask yourself: has it got something to do with what I need to find out?

1   Decide which of these items of information are most and least relevant. For each item in the list, give it a relevance rating on the scale below. Then **make a note** of why you have given it this rating.

1	2	3	4	5

Not very
relevant to Ben

Very relevant
to Ben

a) popular in nightclubs in Ibiza

f) batteries are not included

b) the battery pack is detachable

g) contains an inner pocket

c) small = 85cm

d) £19.95

h) only available in small

e) black cotton

Here is an example: a) = 2. not v. relevant 'cos not wearing it in nightclubs

2   Compare your responses with a partner to see how far you agree on your relevance choices and reasons.

Reinforce your skills

Use the T-Qualizer text to complete the activities below. Remember to practise the skill steps you have just learnt, which help you to:

● skim and scan a text and make a note of relevant information

● explain what those details show you.

1   a) Ben does not get much pocket money each week. Find one piece of information from the Features section of the text which might mean that the T-Qualizer does not suit Ben.

    b) Find one piece of information from the Features section which shows that the T-Qualizer would suit Ben.

2 Ben doesn't wash his own clothes, and his parents don't want him to buy anything that cannot just be put in the washing machine, hung out to dry and ironed easily. What information shows that this shirt will **not** be easy to look after? Give reasons for your answer.

Stretch

Find at least two pieces of evidence in the T-Qualizer text which show that the advertiser is mainly trying to sell the T-Qualizer to people who are interested in clubbing. What different details might have been included if the T-Qualizer was being sold to children?

3 Which of the statements below are true and which are false? Make a note of details from the text which can help you to explain why your point of view is sensible.

- The T-Qualizer is meant for people who enjoy technology.

- The T-Qualizer should never be worn abroad.

- The T-Qualizer will only work with batteries.

- The T-Qualizer is available in three sizes: Small, Medium and Large.

- The T-Qualizer should only be worn by people aged 10+.

Support

Try using these abbreviations in your notes:

∵ = because

& = and

∴ = therefore

You can also abbreviate words, e.g.
lights **&** sound act. dive **&** EL panel.
Make sure you will still know what your notes mean later.

4 So has Ben found the right T-shirt? Discuss your opinion with a partner and explain how you reached your decision.

Extend your skills

You have now practised **scanning** and **skimming** a text to find the information you need. How can you write effectively about the information you find? When you write your answer you need to:

- think carefully about what the evidence is showing you

- quote or refer to the words that prove your point

- write down your point of view

- explain how the evidence you picked out from the text proves your point.

This activity will help you to practise these essential skills.

Below is an extract from the fantasy novel *The Hitch Hiker's Guide to the Galaxy* by Douglas Adams. Complete the activities on the next page to help you work out what each of these places is like by scanning the text and thinking carefully about what it tells you.

a) Jaglan Beta

d) Traal

b) River Moth

e) Santraginus V

c) Kakrafoon

GLOSSARY

interstellar hitch hiker – a hitch hiker who travels between stars
vapours – gases
noxious – harmful

The Hitch Hiker's Guide to the Galaxy has a few things to say on the subject of towels.

A towel, it says, is about the most massively useful thing an interstellar hitch hiker can have. Partly it has great practical value – you can wrap it around you for warmth as you bound across the cold moons of Jaglan Beta; you can lie on it on the brilliant marble-sanded beaches of Santraginus V, inhaling the heady sea vapours; you can sleep under it beneath the stars which shine so redly on the desert world of Kakrafoon; use it to sail a mini raft down the slow heavy river Moth: wet it for use in hand-to-hand combat; wrap it round your head to ward off noxious fumes or avoid the gaze of the Ravenous Bugblatter Beast of Traal (a mindbogglingly stupid animal, it assumes that if you can't see it, it can't see you – daft as a brush, but very, very ravenous); you can wave your towel in emergencies as a distress signal, and of course dry yourself off with it if it still seems clean enough.

Use the steps you learned earlier in this unit to help you to scan the text and find evidence that tells you what the places are like. Fill in a copy of the table below to help you to think through what you want to say about each piece of evidence you have picked out.

1 Sum up what the text tells you about each place. Write this in the **Point** column.

2 Copy exactly what the text says about the place into the **Evidence** column.

3 Think about what each word of the evidence means and suggests. In the **Exploration** column note down what you think the writer is showing you about the place and how this makes you feel.
When you write in the **Evidence** and **Exploration** columns, you should include quotations or refer to specific details in the text. When you want to quote from a text you should:

- place a quotation mark at the beginning of the words you are copying

- copy down the words and punctuation exactly as they appear in the text

- at the end of the words quoted close the quotation marks.

Point What is the text telling me?	Evidence What is the evidence for this in the text?	Exploration What does the evidence show me about the place? How does it make me feel?
Jaglan Beta has cold moons.	'you can wrap it around you for warmth as you bound across the cold moons of Jaglan Beta'	This shows it has more than one moon, but we don't know how many. These moons sound fun because the writer uses the word 'bound' to describe how you can move across them. If the moons are cold, then Jaglan Beta might be too. So, I wouldn't like to go there because I hate being cold.

Stretch

Look at each piece of evidence you chose. Underline the **fewest** words from that sentence which will still prove your point. These are the words you will actually quote in your answer.

Apply your learning

Working on your own, read the text opposite and then complete the task below. Remember to use and explain brief quotations from the text to show that your ideas are sensible.

Task Imagine that you work for a London Tourist Information Centre. You need to reply to the emails below to help these people decide whether or not to visit the Science of Spying exhibition. Read the exhibition review opposite, which is from *Time Out*. First, find the relevant information in the review and make notes that will help you to reply. Then, write the three emails. The opening of the email you should send to Annie has been provided to start you off.

> Hi
>
> I'm visiting from America and am worried it might be pouring with rain when I'm in London. I will need to take the kids (aged 2 and 4) somewhere they can run around, let off steam and enjoy trying out some new stuff. I've heard there's something about spying going on at the Science Museum. Should I go?
>
> Annie

From: Dave Adams
To: Annie Smith
Subject: **Science Museum**
Date: 28 August 2007 13:15:56 BDT

Dear Annie

I have checked out the *Time Out* review on The Science of Spying Exhibition and I do not think it would be very suitable for your young children. The exhibition...

> Dear Sir
>
> I'm going to be looking after my two grandsons aged 9 and 11. They're lively lads and are always pretending to be someone called 'Young Bond'. They'll need to have plenty to do without us having to walk for hours. I can't walk too far these days so I need to take them somewhere with good tube and bus links. I was thinking of taking them to the Science Museum because they might learn something useful! What do you think?
>
> Yours sincerely
>
> Bert Applegate

> Hi
>
> My headteacher has asked me to set up a project for our Year 7 students that involves doing work on the same theme in different subjects. It would be great if we could start with a day out somewhere, but it can't be anywhere too expensive. It needs to be on a topic that 11–12 year olds will enjoy and the trip will need to include lots of different activities if it's going to keep them interested. I was wondering about the Science of Spying Exhibition. Do you think it would be suitable?
>
> Best wishes
>
> Camilla Grey

The Science of Spying

John O'Connell, Issue 1904, Feb 14–20 2007, reproduced courtesy of Time Out London © Time Out, London 2007

Venue: Science Museum, Exhibition Road, London, SW7 2DD

Phone: booking: 0870 906 3890

Category: Museums

Times: tickets are timed and during busy periods your stay is restricted to 1 hour 15 minutes

Price: £8, concs £6, family ticket £18 (1 adult, 2 children) or £25 (2 adults, 2 children); during school holidays and half terms £10/£8/£23/£32

Tube: ⊖ South Kensington

The phenomenal success of Charlie Higson's Young Bond books suggests today's pre-teens find spying every bit as exciting as previous generations of kids.

'The Science of Spying' at the Science Museum is an interactive exhibition focusing on the 'human skills' associated with spying. 'The idea is that you enter as an ordinary civilian but leave as a spy,' says Anna Flaherty. Bearing your personal spy ID card, you enter via secret doors disguised as newspaper and flower sellers' stalls and find yourself in the 'recruitment' area. Here, you stand facing your opponent at the controls of computer consoles resembling Space Invaders machines and test your ability to lie convincingly as you ask and answer questions relating to the pictures you see on the screen. You can also test the steadiness of your hand as you handle a stick of dynamite; learn about disguises and how to use a basic code; and choose the items you want to take with you on your mission.

A single story runs through the exhibition. A sinister company called Ostek is up to mischief. Can you break into it, work out what it's up to and stop its cunning plan for world domination?

The 'recruitment' room leads into the 'technology' room. Here, kids can make 3D maps of their faces or sit on enormous glowing computer keys which vibrate Morse code while adults look at a collection of the latest spy equipment, from lightweight spy-planes to keystroke loggers, RFID tags and 'smart water', which leaves an invisible stain on your skin.

In the next room, Ostek's Security HQ, you undergo further screening before – if you're smart – putting together the final pieces of the puzzle. On the way out you can examine an assortment of surveillance and counter-surveillance gadgets likely to be used by the security services in the near future. (The organisers invited techno-boffin designers to submit ideas and sketches.)

It's all good fun, and certainly shows kids the perils and pleasures of life in our surveillance-obsessed society, even if, at the end of the day, it's more interested in promoting 'enquiry skills' and touching cross-curricular bases (design and technology, ICT, drama, English) than in anything resembling hard science.

It's hard to imagine a ten-year-old who won't love 'The Science of Spying', though parents wanting tales of the Cold War or Bletchley Park might want to head for the Imperial War Museum.

Assess to Progress

How good are you now at each of these skills?

- Locating the main points from texts written in different formats.

- Picking out relevant information in a text.

- Making relevant notes when gathering information.

- Making effective comments on a text.

1   Work with a partner. Look back at the original ratings you gave yourself on page 69. Look at each of the ratings in turn and decide whether any of them should change, using the scale below.

1	2	3	4	5	6	7

I find this difficult.   I'm getting there.   I'm good at this.

2   Use the work you have done in this unit to prove to your partner that your ratings need to change. For example:

> I've done well at reading in different formats because in this unit I've found information in a magazine article, a novel, a web page and emails as well as off the pages of this text book. I think I deserve an excellent now!

3   When do you use these skills outside school? Try to find other opportunities to practise the skills you have developed in this unit.

Look at the timetable below and answer these questions.

1   Which was the first train to leave this morning for Clacton?

2   Which is the next train?

3   How many more trains are there in the next hour?

4   How many trains on the timetable require changes of trains?

5   Which is the longest journey time?

6   Your friend is coming from London to meet you in Clacton-On-Sea
    in Essex. They are at Liverpool Street Station and have texted you
    to ask which train they should catch. They would prefer to have the
    shortest journey possible with no changes. It is now 7am. Write a
    text message giving advice about which train to get, explaining why
    this is the best option.

	buying tickets	help	my account	**Timetable Results**

step 1 of 7

Below is a list of the train departure times which match your outward and return journeys. You can use
the Find earlier trains and Find later trains buttons to click through the rest of the timetable.

Once you have found the times you want, you can book them online. Please click on the Check
Availability and Pricing button below. Or else provide us with more details of the journey by first filling in
the form below.

Outward journey: Tuesday 28 August 2007

Option	1	2	3	4	5
Depart	5:25	06:02	06:25	07:08	07:38
Arrive	07:00	07:36	08:09	08:37	09:34
Changes	0	0	1	0	2
Duration	1:34	1:34	1:44	1:29	1:56
Details	view	view	view	view	view

Find earlier trains   **Find later trains**

Return journey: Tuesday 29 August 2007

Option	1	2	3	4	5
Depart	12:50	13:50	14:50		
Arrive	14:16	15:16	16:16		
Changes	0	0	0		
Duration	1:26	1:26	1:26		
Details	view	view	view		

Find earlier trains   **Find later trains**

If your booking includes a tube journey and you are travelling late at night or early in the morning you
can check the opening and closing times of the stations at London Underground or at Manchester
Metrolink

Check availability and pricing for these times.

If you would like to purchase a ticket based on the times above please enter your journey details below
and click the Check Availability and Pricing button

Who is going?

Number of Adults: 1   Number of children: (aged 5 to 15)   0

What type of railcard: [▼]   (only one railcard can be used per booking)

Reading AF3
Progress in ... Using inference and deduction

LEARNING OBJECTIVES

- Understand a text's literal meaning (what it says on the surface).
- Use inference and deduction to recognise implicit meanings. This means using clues to work out what a writer means when you are not told directly.
- Give a personal response to the texts you read.

Activate your learning

Read this eyewitness account of a crime that may have been committed, then complete the activities on the next page.

6"0
5"6
5"0
4"6
4"0
3"6
3"0

I was hanging about near the library waiting for the bus that takes me home. It's the number 47 and usually runs at the top and bottom of each hour. It was about 4:40 and I'd been there five minutes. There was no sign of a bus, but I did notice a bloke in a baseball cap hanging around near the back door to the library. The library was still open and I could see mums with toddlers and other people going in and out through the main entrance. He was in a white tracksuit, smoking, and didn't look like he worked there. He looked as if he was waiting for something or someone. There was something about him that made me not want him to see that I was watching him, so I listened to my MP3 player and pretended to be lost in a world of my own. Suddenly the back door opened slightly, a hand came out holding a bag, the bloke in white took it, threw his cigarette down and started walking very quickly away from the library. He walked into the main street, pulled his baseball cap down over his eyes and disappeared into the crowd. That's when I decided to phone you.

1 Rate each of these statements as:
- Definitely true (clear evidence in the text)
- Probably true (hinted at in the text)
- Untrue (factually incorrect)
- No evidence to know this.

Statements
a) The writer was waiting near the library
b) The writer has contacted the police
c) The writer is male
d) The writer's bus was number 47
e) The writer's bus was late
f) The suspect was wearing a white tracksuit
g) The suspect was male
h) The suspect was behaving suspiciously
i) The suspect was menacing
j) The suspect was handling stolen goods

2 a) Think of a reason for the suspect's behaviour that is completely innocent and not at all suspicious.

b) Think of a reason why the writer might want to make the suspect seem suspicious.

Assess to Progress

How well can you read on the surface and between the lines already?

Rate yourself for each skill by deciding which number on the scale below best shows your skill level.

1   2   3   4   5   6   7

I find this difficult.   I'm getting there.   I'm good at this.

- I can easily understand the surface (literal) level of most texts I read.

  Self-check: You pick up a text at random – a newspaper, leaflet, novel or magazine. Would you be able to list the main points covered on one page of it?

- I can read between the lines of most texts by using clues the writer gives to work out what is meant.

  Self-check: You've read a novel where the writer keeps you guessing about which characters to trust. Can you spot the clues?

- I can give my personal response to most texts, supporting what I say with evidence from the text.

  Self-check: You've finished the book and now you need to write a personal response which explains your views. Can you do it?

Build your skills

She even went on television, in a special show to talk about herself and her medal,

You can understand texts better and enjoy them more if you are able to use **inference** and **deduction** to read between the lines. You can use this skill with all sorts of texts. The best picture books for young children allow the reader to use clues in the pictures to find out more about the characters and story.

and the cups she had won for being polite, being spotless, being helpful, being best at sums, reading, poetry and writing.

Look at the two pages from *Super Dooper Jezebel* by Tony Ross. Aimed at very young readers, he describes a girl who seems to be perfect: at school, at home and at everything!

Step 1 Read on the surface to find the literal meaning

1 Name one thing that Jezebel goes on television to show she is good at.

2 How many people in the picture are watching her on television?

3 How many cups has she won?

Step 2 Read beneath the surface to find the implied meaning

1 Look more closely at the picture of Jezebel on the television holding her medal. Choose which of these words best describes her:

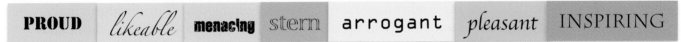

PROUD   *likeable*   **menacing**   stern   **arrogant**   *pleasant*   INSPIRING

2 Look at the people watching the television. How much is Jezebel impressing them?

3 Look at the image of Jezebel showing off her trophies. Focus on her face. What impression do you get of her?

Step 3 Give a personal response

1 The text of the story suggests that Jezebel is an excellent role model. The pictures give us a slightly different view of her. In your own words, write a paragraph describing what you notice about Super Dooper Jezebel. You should refer to evidence from the story in your response. Look for details that will help to support your comments.

> ### Support
> You could use the following phrases to help you to refer to evidence from the story:
> - I notice that ...
> - In the text Jezebel seems ...
> - In the images Jezebel seems ...
> - There is a contrast between ...

Reinforce your skills

You are now going to practise reading for surface and beneath-the-surface meanings in the opening of Anthony Horowitz's novel, *Raven's Gate*. See what you notice.

Matt Freeman knew he was making a mistake.

He was sitting on a low wall outside Ipswich station, wearing a grey hooded sweatshirt, shapeless, faded jeans, and trainers with frayed laces. It was six o'clock in the evening and the London train had just pulled in. Behind him, commuters were fighting their way out of the station. The concourse was a tangle of cars, taxis and pedestrians, all of them trying to find their way home. A traffic light blinked from red to green but nothing moved. Somebody leant on their horn and the noise blared out, cutting through the damp evening air. Matt heard it and looked up briefly. But the crowd meant nothing to him. He wasn't part of it. He never had been – and he sometimes thought he never would be.

Two men carrying umbrellas walked past and glanced at him disapprovingly. They probably thought he was up to no good. The way he was sitting – hunched

forward with his knees apart – made him look somehow dangerous, and older than fourteen. He had broad shoulders, a well-developed, muscular body and bright blue, intelligent eyes. His hair was black, cut very short. Give him another five years and he could be a footballer or a model – or, like plenty of others, both.

His first name was Matthew but he always called himself Matt. As the troubles had begun to pile up in his life, he had used his surname less and less until it was no longer a part of him. Freeman was the name on the school register and on the truancy list, and it was a name well known to the local social services. But Matthew never wrote it down and seldom spoke it. 'Matt' was enough. The name suited him. After all, for as long as he could remember, people had been walking all over him.

He watched the two men with umbrellas cross the bridge and disappear in the direction of the city centre. Matt hadn't been born in Ipswich. He had been brought here and he hated everything about the place. For a start, it wasn't a city. It was too small. But it had none of the charm of a village or a market town. It was really just an oversized shopping centre with the same shops and supermarkets that you saw everywhere else. You could swim in the Crown Pools or you could see movies at the multiplex – or, if you could afford it, there was an artificial ski slope and go-karting. But that was about it. It didn't even have a decent football team.

1   Working with a partner or on your own, create a spider diagram
     labelled 'Surface meaning' and write down eight details the writer tells
     us about Ipswich station.

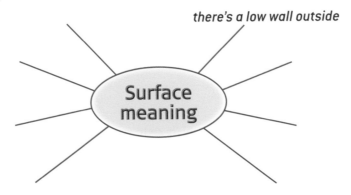

there's a low wall outside

Surface
meaning

2   Now focus on the character of Matt. For each of the statements about
     Matt below, decide whether we are told this directly, whether it is
     hinted at or whether there is no evidence.

Information	We are told this directly	This is hinted at	There is no evidence for this
a) Matthew likes to be called 'Matt'.	✔		
b) Matt's surname is 'Freeman'.			
c) Matt is fourteen.			
d) Matt is observant.			
e) Matt senses something strange is happening.			
f) Matt is unhappy with his life.			
g) Matt has short black hair.			
h) Matt dislikes living in Ipswich.			
i) Matt has a sense of humour.			
j) Matt has strong opinions.			

3   Which of the statements did you find it most difficult to decide on?
     Why? Compare your responses with a partner's.

4 a) Now think about your own response to the text. How effective is the opening of the novel? Does it grab your attention and make you want to keep reading?

b) Look at this response written by Josh. Think about what works well and where he could make improvements. What advice would you give him about how he could improve it?

I quite like the opening sentence of the novel. It gets my interest and gets me wanting to read on. To be honest I think Matt Freeman sounds like a bit of a whinger because all he seems to do is moan about everything such as where he lives, the fact that it's too small and even its football team. This means he's not a very nice character at the start but I like the way he feels like the whole world is on his shoulders and he kind of feels picked on. I also think it seems sort of a boy's book.

Support

Think about these questions when you are commenting on Josh's work.

Content (what it's about)
- Does he cover the whole extract?
- Does he talk about character, place and plot (storyline)?
- Does he leave out any important details?
- Does he make fair points about the story?
- Does he refer to details from the text to support his views?

Style (how it's written)
- Does he write clearly?
- Does he repeat himself?
- Are there any words that he could change for better ones?
- Could his style be more or less formal?

Stretch

Redraft Josh's response so that it makes more precise points, supporting these with relevant evidence from the text.
Then write two or three sentences describing how you redrafted it and why.

Extend your skills

You are now going to develop your skills in using **inference** and **deduction** to read between the lines, this time with a non-fiction text.

Bear Grylls is an adventurer and explorer who presents survival programmes on television. In this extract from an article in *The Times* newspaper Matt Dickinson describes a moment during filming in the Alps.

Read the text and complete the tasks on the next page.

Into the **lair** of the **bear**

It is 6.15am, five degrees below freezing, and I'm 2,400m (7,870ft) above sea level. We are gathered, shivering and nervous, next to a frozen lake. Bear is going to look for thin ice. He wants to show us how to escape this potential death trap. The main camera has just blacked out with frozen condensation on the lens. I can feel the linings in my nose crackling every time I take a breath. Inside my Gore-Tex suit I can feel my bones chilling fast.

Bear strips off to his T-shirt and walks out on to the ice. There are ominous cracking noises, but Bear is unconcerned. He looks like a chap off for a Sunday-afternoon stroll.

Ravens gather like vultures on an icy pinnacle above the lake. Bear takes the leap. There is an explosion of fractured ice as he plunges into the water. He starts his piece to camera. A minute passes. Bear's lips turn blue. I can see blood welling from the scratches where the ice has lacerated his arm. Hypothermia is kicking in and his speech slows. I'm worried we may be filming Bear's last moments. Then he's kicking out. Serious muscle power is called into play and Bear scrambles up on to the ice. He stands shaking, a quivering mass of superchilled flesh. 'How was that?' he asks. 'Can I do it again?'

GLOSSARY

Gore-Tex suit – protective clothing worn in extreme weather conditions
hypothermia – dangerously low body temperature
lacerated – torn, wounded
ominous – threatening
pinnacle – a high pointed rock
welling – rising to the surface

1 Imagine you are a teacher asking students to respond to this text. Think of two questions you might ask to see whether they have understood the literal (surface) meaning. Write down your questions and the answers.

2 Now explore some of the implied meanings in this article.
   a) From reading the text, decide which of these words best describes Matt's opinion of Bear. Support your choice with evidence from the text.

admiration   fear   worry   protectiveness   dislike   disbelief   friendship

   b) Now explore the way that Matt's feelings shift during the three paragraphs. Look at the graph below and, for each paragraph, plot where you think Matt's emotions should be by placing a number 1, 2 and 3 in the position that you think best sums up his emotions. Compare your graph with a partner's.

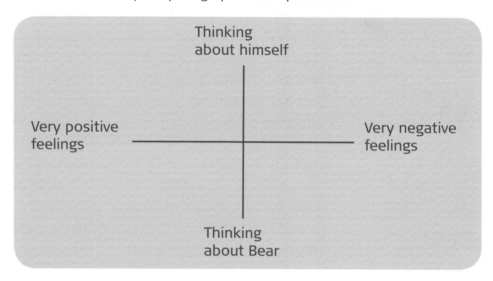

3 How tense and exciting do you find the article? Remember to support what you say with evidence from the text.

Stretch

A good writer can choose words that give different or additional meanings to help deliver the text's overall theme or message. For example, Matt Dickinson writes:

'The main camera has just blacked out with frozen condensation on the lens.'

Why do you think we used the phrase 'blacked out' here? When would you usually use this phrase? How does this link with the overall theme of the text?

Apply your learning

In 1972 a plane carrying a rugby team from Chile crashed high in the remote Andes mountains. Many of the passengers were killed, but the survivors included Nando Parrado, who lay unconscious for three days following the crash.

Working on your own, read this extract from Nando's autobiography where he describes how he felt as he regained consciousness and realised the terrible situation he was in. Nando's mother and sister were killed in the crash and the avalanche that followed, and here he describes his desperation to get back home to his father. Then complete the task on the next page.

GLOSSARY

vulnerability – feeling very insecure
grim – gloomy
manic – mad

In my desperation, I raged silently at the great peaks that loomed above the crash site, blocking the path to my father, and trapping me in this evil place. Frustration gnawed at me until, like a man buried alive, I began to panic. Every moment that passed was filled with one fear, as if the earth beneath my feet were a ticking bomb that might explode at any second. This terrifying sense of vulnerability – the certainty that doom was only moments away – never rested. It filled every moment of my time on the mountain and it produced in me a manic urge to flee. I fought this fear the best I could, trying to calm myself and think clearly, but there were moments when animal instinct threatened to overcome reason, and it would take all my strength to keep from bolting off blindly into the mountain range.

At first, the only way I could quiet these fears was to picture in my mind the moment when rescuers would arrive to save us, but as time passed I could not silence the doubts that were growing in my mind. We had always assumed that the authorities knew roughly where our plane had gone down. They must have known our route through the mountains, we told ourselves, and surely the pilots had radioed along the way. It would simply be a matter of searching along the flight path, beginning at the point of the last radio contact. How hard could it be to spot the wreckage of a large aeroplane lying in plain view on an open glacier?

But surely, I thought, a concentrated search would have found us by now? And the fact that rescue hadn't come forced me to consider two grim conclusions: either they had a mistaken idea of where we had fallen, and were searching some other stretch of the mountain range, or, they had no idea at all where in the sprawling mountains we might be. I remembered the wildness of the mountains as we flew through them, all those steep-walled ravines plunging thousands of feet along the slopes of so many black, winding ridges, and nothing but more slopes and ridges as far as the eye could see. These thoughts forced me to a grim conclusion: They haven't found us yet because they have no idea where we are, and if they don't know even roughly where we are, they will never find us.

Task **Understanding the text**

1 Why does Nando 'rage against the mountains'?

2 What does Nando mean when he says it felt as if there were a 'ticking bomb' beneath his feet?

3 How do Nando's feelings about the chance of rescue change?

Responding to the implied meaning in the text

4 How can we tell that Nando has to work hard to control his feelings?

5 What impression do you get of Nando's state of mind?

6 How does the writer make the sense of horror seem very strong?

Personal response

7 Write two paragraphs about your response to the text. In the **first** paragraph, describe how you react to Nando, e.g. what you notice about how he copes, what his thoughts and feelings are and how he expresses himself.

In the **second** paragraph, say what you think about the text, e.g. which parts interest you, how it is structured, how the writer creates drama and holds our interest and whether the text makes you wish to read on.

Assess to Progress

Work with a partner. Read each other's answers to the questions in the Apply your learning section. Then look back at the original ratings you gave yourself on page 81 for each of these skills and see if any can change.

1	2	3	4	5	6	7

I find this difficult.   I'm getting there.   I'm good at this.

- I easily understand the surface (literal) level of most texts I read.
  Self-check: How well do you think you answered questions 1–3?

- I can use inference and deduction to read between the lines to work out meanings in most texts.
  Self-check: How easy did you find it to answer questions 4–6?

- I can give my personal response to most texts and support what I say with evidence from the text.
  Self-check: Did your response to question 7 cover each of the points?

You have opened a bank account with a well-known bank. Suddenly you receive this email:

> **"Account Status Notification"**
>
> We are contacting you to remind you that our Account Review Team identified some unusual activity in your account. In accordance with our Online Banking User Agreement and to ensure that your account has not been accessed from fraudulent locations, for your security, We placed extra verification on your Online Access until this issue has been resolved please log in your account by clicking on the link below: Once you log in your account details, You will be automatically redirected to our online Legal Releases.
>
> *Online Security Department*

You aren't sure whether the message is genuine or designed to obtain your personal details.

1 What clues are there on the surface that the message may be genuine?

2 What clues are there when you study the text more closely that it may be a fake?

3 What would you do if you received this email?

Progress in ... Analysing how texts are organised and structured

LEARNING OBJECTIVES

- Recognise some ways in which different texts are organised.
  This means how the writer presents the text and organises the ideas in it.
- Identify some different techniques for organising ideas.
- Evaluate how structural choices support the purpose of a text.

Activate your learning

1 Read the five texts on the opposite page. There is one of each of the following types of text. Which do you think is which?

| diary | poem | newspaper story | encyclopaedia entry | novel |

2 The writers of these texts have shared some of their thoughts about how they have organised their writing. Read the thought bubbles below and decide who wrote which text.

I am writing about events in time order. I begin a new paragraph whenever there is a new topic or person, or when someone speaks.

1

2

I make a general statement first. Then I give different examples, where I can go into detail. Bullet points set out the information clearly for the reader.

3

I am writing according to a pattern or formula. I have to think about the sounds of the words and the lengths of the lines.

4

I am writing about events in time order. The headings show when each sequence of events happened.

5

I begin with a heading to grab the reader's attention. Then I use short paragraphs. The first paragraph describes the main point that I am making.

A

I took a deep breath and opened the door. The room reeked of teenage boy, that odour of socks and stale air and leftover takeaway. I couldn't tell you what colour the carpet was because it was invisible under piles of magazines, **CD** cases, schoolbooks, dirty clothes and pizza boxes.

I was about to enter when I heard footsteps coming up the stairs.

'Who's there?' It was Ben, and he was angry.

B

There was a teenager from Tring
Who suddenly thought she could sing
She went on X Factor
But quickly they sacked her
That deluded teenager from Tring.

C

Coming of age ceremonies

In many cultures there are special ceremonies that celebrate the moment when a child becomes an adult:

- Upanayanam is a coming of age ceremony for males in the Hindu world.
- In Judaism, 12-year-old females and 13-year-old males become b'nai mitzvah and often have a celebration to mark this coming of age.
- In the United States, girls will often have a 'sweet sixteen' party to celebrate turning 16.

D

<u>Monday 13 May</u>
Sal arrived at the door before I finished breakfast and Mum made me take the toast with me to the bus stop because apparently you'll die of something nasty if you only eat half a slice for breakfast. I hate her since of course HE was there and there's me with my mouth full of crumbs and a doorstep of wholemeal toast and jam in my sticky hand. So not cool.

<u>Tuesday 14 May</u>
He was there again today.

E

OFF THE STREETS

A new survey shows that only two out of ten children play on their local streets. When their parents were kids, this figure was seven out of ten. The biggest reason given for children no longer playing in the streets was the level of traffic. The survey was carried out for Playday 2007. The director of Playday England said, 'The modern world is making streets a no-go zone for children.'

Assess to Progress

How well can you comment on the ways texts are organised?

Copy the grid below and tick the relevant box next to each skill. Be as honest as you can. This will help you set targets for your learning in this unit. If you need help, think about how well you performed in the activity on the previous page.

I can ...	Easily	Sometimes	Not very often
Recognise some ways different texts are organised			
Identify some different techniques for organising ideas			
Explain how the ideas in a text are organised			

Build your skills

On the opposite page is a humorous text about looking after children. Read the text, then discuss the following questions about the text to help you to think about how effectively it has been organised.

1 The main heading gives readers their first clue about what is going on.

   a) Headings are often designed to make you want to read on. Does this one do that?

   b) The line underneath the heading (the **strapline**) has a slightly different purpose. Complete this sentence: 'The strapline explains ...'

2 The text is divided up into smaller blocks or paragraphs. How does this help the reader?

3 Each paragraph has a heading, but five are incomplete. Work out which of these phrases is the right one to fill each gap.

Dressing	Shopping	Feeding	Sleeping	Toy

4 The writing in each paragraph follows a very similar pattern. Can you spot it? Hint: look at the words that begin each sentence. Why do you think the writer has used this technique?

5 Do you usually expect a text giving you instructions to be funny? How does structuring the text in this way add to the humour?

Are you ready for children?

Try these simple tests to see how prepared you are to be a parent!

Mess Test

Smear peanut butter on the sofa and curtains. Now rub your hands in the wet flowerbed and rub on the walls. Cover the stains with crayons. Place a fish finger behind the couch and leave it there all summer.

_____ Test

Obtain a big box of Lego. Spread pieces all over the house. Put on a blindfold. Try to walk to the bathroom or kitchen. Do not scream. (This could wake a child at night.)

_____ Test

Obtain a large plastic milk jug. Fill halfway with water. Suspend from the ceiling with a strong cord. Start the jug swinging. Try to insert spoonfuls of soggy cereal into the mouth of the jug, while pretending to be an airplane. Now dump the contents of the jug on the floor.

_____ Test

Prepare by obtaining a small cloth bag and fill it with about eight pounds of wet sand. Put in a cot. At 8.00pm pick up the bag and begin to waltz and hum with it until 9.00pm. Lay down your bag and set your alarm for 10.00pm. Get up, pick up your bag, and sing every song you have ever heard. Make up about a dozen more and sing these too until 4.00am. Set alarm for 5.00am. Get up and make breakfast. Keep this up for five years. Look cheerful.

_____ Test

Obtain one large, unhappy, live octopus. Stuff into a small bag, making sure that all arms stay inside.

_____ Test

Borrow one or two lively goats and take them with you as you shop at the supermarket. Always keep them in sight and pay for anything they eat or damage.

Reinforce your skills

The following extract is from the opening of *Deeper than Colour,* a short story by Ijeoma Inyama.

1   As you read, think about the way the author has organised the text. Working in pairs, discuss the questions around the text.

1   What is the first paragraph about? Hint: read the opening sentence carefully.

God! Miss Halpern, our English teacher, is well renk! She reckons our class would be '*much more productive*' if we weren't sat with our friends. So she moves us about and makes us sit with people she *knows* we'd never sit with through choice. She's vex me *twice,* man! First of all you don't expect to get treated like a Year seven when you're in Year eleven – I mean, her idea of seating arrangement is well antiquated! And secondly, she's taken me away from my spars, man. Ever since Year eight I've sat next to Heather Phillips, in front of Antoinette Varley and Takesha Brown. Now barely into the first term of Year eleven and we get split up!

2   These words help to put the events in order of *when* they happened. Where else in this paragraph has the writer used words like this to organise the text?

3   Why has the author begun a new paragraph here?

'Nadine Charles, I want you to sit next to John Danucci in front of my desk.'

Now she's vexed me four times, no make that five. Sitting next to Danucci *and* in the front row. I can't believe it! Neither can the rest of the class. *Everyone* knows we're the worst pairing ever.

He hangs out with the 'trendies'. We call them the *Kiss FM posse.* They're into 'British soul' and buy their clothes from 'Hyper' – anything that's the latest t'ing. I mean, if it was thrashing two dustbin lids together, them lot'd be into that, no danger.

4   Is this paragraph about Danucci or the trendies? Does this explain why the author has begun a new paragraph here?

2   Write a short sentence to sum up what each of the four paragraphs is about.

3   The author has organised these paragraphs in several different ways:

● by time sequence (telling the reader what happened when)

● by topic (grouping information about a particular topic together)

● by direct speech (to show what somebody is saying).

a) Look back at the extract and decide how each paragraph has been organised.

b) How does the opening prepare the reader for what the rest of the story is about? What do you think will happen next?

Extend your skills

Below is the text for a newspaper story about a teenager whose new job is to play computer games. It has not been organised into paragraphs.

1   In pairs, decide how to separate the text into paragraphs. Remember how newspaper stories are organised:

- Short paragraphs, of one or two sentences only, are used to keep the reader's attention.

- A new person, topic or fact is given a new paragraph.

- Whenever anyone is quoted, their words go in a new paragraph.

A teenager has landed a job travelling the world playing computer games. Pete Wright, 19, is Britain's top player at shoot 'em up Counter-Strike: Source. Software bosses were so impressed they signed him up to demonstrate the game at international tournaments. His first task is to compete in the Los Angeles world finals next month for a share of the £245,000 prize money. Pete, from Plymouth, whose salary is £14,700, said yesterday. 'It's a dream come true. I get paid money to play.'

2   Compare your ideas with those of another pair. If they are different, discuss which is the more likely organisation for the text and why.

3   Work in pairs to choose the best **headline** and the best **strapline** for the newspaper article from those shown below.

Teen paid to play computer games

Strike it lucky

Gunning for glory

Plymouth teenager lands dream job playing computer games

Teenager chosen to demonstrate games for top software company

British teen to take on world at computer game tournament

Support

Remember, a headline should grab the reader's attention. The strapline should explain a bit more about the story.

Stretch

Write a short statement explaining why you think your combination of headline and strapline is best. Think about what effect your choice would have on the reader.

Apply your learning

The text on the opposite page is taken from the BBC Parenting website and gives advice to parents of teenagers. Use the skills you have developed in this unit so far to complete the following task.

Task

1   Look at the layout of the text:

   a) What does the title tell the reader or make them expect?

   b) Why do you think the first paragraph is in bold?

   c) What job are the sub-headings doing?

2   Look at the ways the paragraphs are organised:

   a) What is the main point of each paragraph?

   b) The first sentence of a paragraph often tells you what it is about. This is called a topic sentence. Identify two topic sentences in this text.

   c) Choose two paragraphs and explain how they group related events or information together. How does the way these paragraphs are structured help to support the overall purpose of the text?

3   Look at the introduction entitled 'Appreciating your teen'. The paragraph follows this structure:

   • First it focuses on the bad aspects of teenagers, e.g. 'misdemeanours', 'wild behaviour'.

   • Then it focuses on the good.

   a) How does the whole text echo this structure? Look at the balance between the 'good' and 'bad' aspects of teenagers. Where are these included in the text?

   b) What job does this suggest an introduction can do in a piece of writing?

4   a) Look at the web page as a whole. What other presentational features help to give the reader information about what the text is about?

   b) If a reader wanted to find out more advice about teenage life, which parts of the website would help them?

bbc.co.uk | Home | TV | Radio | Talk | Where I Live | A-Z Index | Search

Lifestyle

bbc.co.uk
BBC **Parenting**

TV and radio | A to Z index | Talk

BBC Homepage
Lifestyle
Parenting
Your kids
Teens
Academic achievement
Appreciating your teen
Bullying
Career choices
Common teenage problems
Communication
Developmental stages
Discipline
Handling failure
Letting go
Peer pressure
Risky behaviour
Sexuality
Truancy

TV and radio
Talk
Newsletter

Appreciating your teen

Teens often get a bad press, and it's chiefly misdemeanours and wild behaviour that are the focus of parent's attention. But by focusing on the bad, you could be missing out on all the good...

Such typical 'teenage' behaviour, such as trying alcohol or drugs, having relationships and staying out late, are only part of the picture. Many of the negative stereotypes attached to adolescence, such as delinquency and violence, are also quite incorrect. A few teenagers may behave in this way, but the vast majority don't.

Living with teenagers

Once your child becomes a teenager, you'll find you have an interesting companion to chat to and share ideas with. You may even discover a new zest for life from the enthusiasm and energy of your teenager – all that optimism can be infectious.

Wise parents learn to respect their children as the adults they'll soon become, while still understanding they may sometimes want to behave in a younger way.

This can be puzzling but, just as in the toddler years, your teen is torn between going all out for independence and swinging back to the familiar security of an earlier age. During stressful times, it can be all too easy to forget that inside your argumentative teenager is your tender child.

Adolescent identity

Throughout his teens, your child is developing his identity. He may lack confidence and worry about his looks, body and the strange feelings and thoughts he's experiencing. Remember – he's sorting things out for himself, not rejecting you. For him growing up involves demonstrating how different he is from the adults around him. He needs to find ways of expressing this difference; he may disagree with everything you say, for example.

Be prepared

Assess to Progress

In this unit you have learned about some of the different ways in which texts are organised to help the reader. How good are you now at each of these skills?

- Recognising some ways in which different texts are organised.
- Identifying some different techniques for organising ideas.
- Explaining how the ideas in a text are organised.

1   Look at the chart that you filled in at the start of the unit. Try it again and see what you have improved on. Use the work that you have done in this unit to prove to your partner that your new ratings are the correct ones.

I can...	Easily	Sometimes	Not very often
Recognise some ways different texts are organised			
Identify some different techniques for organising ideas			
Explain how the ideas in a text are organised			

2   Now complete the sentences below:

I have learned most about ...

I need to learn more about ...

2   Set yourself two targets that will help you to analyse how texts are organised and structured in future work.

SKILLS FOR LIFE

Your local Fire Service wants to update its online advice about fire safety. They particularly want to make the website relevant to your age group, so they have asked your class for advice.

1   Look at the current web page and give feedback on:

   ▶ how the page is organised – be as specific as you can about how all the elements are set out (e.g. titles, navigation bars, images)

   ▶ how the page could be organised to present its message better

   ▶ how you would advise them to make it relevant to your age group.

2   Make a list of the essential information that the web page includes, such as 'Information about what to do when a smoke alarm goes off'. Which piece of information do you think is the most important?

Fireservice
www.fireservice.co.uk

Home > Safety > Home Fire Safety Advice

The Facts.

Every year the fire brigade is called out to over 600,000 fires in the home. And every year around 500 people die in these fires and over 10,000 are injured.

If a fire occurs in your home, your chances of survival will depend on how quickly and safely you can get out. This information will give you advice on how to prevent a fire, and how to protect yourself should one occur.

We all try to prevent fires from starting in the home. But it only takes an unguarded or careless moment for a fire to start. A couple of minutes later and your home could be filled with smoke. Smoke and fumes can kill – particularly the highly poisonous smoke from some furnishings. You will only have a short time to get out. Use it wisely and try not to panic.
If your smoke alarm goes off in the night while you are asleep, do not investigate to see if there is a fire.

• Shout and wake everyone up.
• Get everyone together and make your way out.
• Follow your plan and get out.

Remember it is always better to have a plan which has been discussed with family members beforehand so that in the case of fire every family member is prepared and knows exactly what to do. If possible close the door of the room where the fire is and close all doors behind you as you leave. This will help delay the spread of fire and smoke. Before opening a closed door use the back of your hand to touch it. Don't open it if it feels warm – the fire could be on the other side.

• Get everyone out as quickly as possible.
• Don't try to pick up valuables or possessions.

If there is a lot of smoke crawl with your nose close to the floor, the air should be better and clearer there. If you live on a ground floor then it will be easier to get out. If you need to break a window, do so safely and cover any edges with towels or bedding to cover edges of broken glass. If you need to get out higher than the ground floor then throw some bedding onto the ground to break your fall. Never jump from the window, lower yourself down and then drop at arm's length.

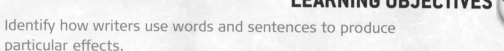

Reading AF5
Progress in ... Analysing how writers use language to shape meaning

LEARNING OBJECTIVES

- Identify how writers use words and sentences to produce particular effects.
- Describe what effects a writer's use of language has.
- Comment on how a writer's language choices have an effect on the reader.

Activate your learning

Read this description of two boys diving in a coral lagoon, taken from the novel *The Coral Island* by R. M. Ballantyne.

> When Jack and I dived into shallower water, we expected to have found sand and stones, instead of which we found ourselves in what appeared really to be an enchanted garden. The whole of the bottom of the lagoon, as we called the calm water within the reef, was covered with coral of every shape, size, and hue. Some portions were formed like large mushrooms; others appeared like the brain of a man, having stalks or necks attached to them; but the most common kind was a species of branching coral, and some portions were of a lovely pale pink colour, others were pure white.

1 Look at the phrases that have been highlighted. With a partner, rank them in order of how well they help you to imagine the scene.

2 Compare your list with another pair. If your lists are different, discuss the reasons why. Try to persuade the other pair that your ranking is the best one. Be open to changing your mind!

3 Look at the phrase that you have at the top of your list. Write a sentence explaining how it helps the reader to imagine what the boys see as they dive.

4 Now look at the length of the sentences. Which sentence is the longest? Why do you think the writer used a long sentence here? Is it:

- to make the writing seem faster

- to slow the writing down

- to add lots of detail and description

- to pack in a lot of information?

Assess to Progress

How good are you already at commenting on how a writer uses language?

Rank yourself on the following scale to say how well you think you can identify how writers use language and what effect their language choices have on the reader.

1	2	3	4	5	6	7

I find this difficult.   I'm getting there.   I'm good at this.

If you need help assessing your skills, think back to the activity above. You can also ask yourself these questions:

- Can I identify effective words and phrases from a passage?

- Can I describe the effect these words and phrases create?

- Can I identify particular techniques a writer uses?

- Can I comment on how a writer's language choices affect the reader?

Build your skills

A pupil has been given the extract below from the novel *Treasure Island* by Robert Louis Stevenson. It describes a character that the narrator, Jim, meets. She has been asked to answer the following question:

How does the writer use language to create a vivid impression of the character Jim meets?

> I remember him as if it were yesterday, as he came plodding to the inn door, his sea-chest following behind him in a hand-barrow; a tall, strong, heavy, nut-brown man; his tarry pigtail falling over the shoulders of his soiled blue coat; his hands ragged and scarred, with black, broken nails; and the sabre cut across one cheek, a dirty, livid white. I remember him looking round the cove and whistling to himself as he did so, and then breaking out in that old sea-song that he sang so often afterwards:
>
> 'Fifteen men on the dead man's chest –
> Yo-ho-ho and a bottle of rum!'

The three skill steps below show you how to comment effectively on a writer's use of language.

Step 1 Identify key words and phrases

Think about which words and phrases stand out and will help you to answer the question. Look at the phrases the pupil has picked out:

'I remember him as if it were yesterday' – *the word 'yesterday' suggests that the picture of him is still fresh in his mind as if he had seen him recently.*

'his hands ragged and scarred ... the sabre cut across one cheek' – *the writer gives us the impression the man has been in lots of fights.*

1   Do you agree that these stand out and help to create a vivid impression of the character? Which other words or phrases could you select?

Step 2 Pick out any techniques that the writer has used to create an effect

Look for examples of techniques such as metaphors, similes, alliteration or lists of adjectives. Think about what effect the use of the technique has. The most important thing is not spotting the technique, but being able to explain how it helps to create an effect.

Look at the list of adjectives the pupil has picked out:

'a tall, strong, heavy, nut-brown man' – *the list of adjectives helps to give a lot of description very quickly.*

1   Do you agree with this explanation of why a list of adjectives has been used? How else has the writer used language to create a vivid impression?

2   Look at the phrase 'black, broken nails'. Here the writer uses alliteration (repeating the 'b' sound at the start of the word) to describe the man's appearance. How does this help to create a vivid impression?

Step 3 Describe what effect the words and phrases have

What do the words and phrases you have picked out suggest to you? What do they make you think about? How do they help to build up a picture in your mind?

Look at what the pupil has written about the word 'soiled'.

'his soiled blue coat' – *the adjective 'soiled' suggests that his coat is mucky or grubby because soil means dirt, so it's not very clean.*

1   Do you think this is a good explanation of the effect this word has? Which other words from the passage also help to create this impression of the man?

> ### Stretch
> What do you notice about the sentence length in the extract? How does this help to build up the description of the man?

2   Using the notes the pupil has made, write a paragraph answering the question: How does the writer use language to create a vivid impression of the character Jim meets?

Reinforce your skills

Good writers use different kinds of sentence structure to produce different effects. The passage below is taken from the novel *Jaws* by Peter Benchley. Here, Hooper goes beneath the surface of the sea in a cage looking for the killer shark that has been preying on swimmers.

Read the passage carefully, then use the three skill steps you have learnt to help you answer the questions, which explore the use of sentences for different effects.

GLOSSARY

darkling – obscure, gloomy
ferrous – iron-coloured
incalculable – beyond calculation, very great
serrate – notched like a saw
pectoral – on the chest

1 Putting Hooper's name at the beginning of the sentence makes this character the focus of the sentence. Pick out two more examples of this type of sentence. Look at the second sentence – how is this different?

3 The writer could have written: 'The top of the immense body was a hard ferrous grey. It was bluish where dappled with streaks of sun.' What is the effect of writing a single longer sentence?

6 What makes this sentence different from the ones just before it? If you set it to music, how loud and fast would it be?

Hooper glanced downward, started to look away, then snapped his eyes down again. Rising at him from the darkling blue – <u>slowly, smoothly</u> – was the shark. It rose with no apparent effort, an angel of death gliding towards an appointment.

Hooper stared, enthralled, impelled to flee but unable to move. As the fish drew nearer, he marvelled at its colours: the flat brown-greys seen on the surface had vanished. The top of the immense body was a hard ferrous grey, bluish where dappled with streaks of sun. The fish came closer, silent as a shadow, and Hooper drew back. The head was only a few feet from the cage when the fish turned and began to pass before Hooper's eyes – casually, as if in proud display of its incalculable mass and power. The snout passed first, then the jaw, slack and smiling, armed with row upon row of serrate triangles. And then the black, fathomless eye, seemingly riveted upon him. The fish began to turn, banking, the rubbery pectoral fins changing pitch.

The fish rammed through the space between the bars.

2 The words 'slowly, smoothly' in the middle of this sentence have the effect of slowing down the reader's discovery that this is a shark so it builds suspense.

4 This long sentence slows the action down. Why do you think the writer wanted to do that here?

5 This sentence doesn't have a proper verb (action word). What does this make the sentence emphasise?

Whenever you are asked to comment on a writer's use of language you should not only focus on individual words and phrases, but also look at the types of sentences they've used and the way these are structured. Remember the most important thing is to explain what effect is created.

Extend your skills

As you've seen from using the skill steps to explore a **writer's use of language**, sometimes it helps to use special terms to describe the techniques that writers use.

1   Read the following passage, also from *Jaws*, with a partner and find an example of each of the techniques listed below it.

> The sea was as flat as gelatine. There was no whisper of wind to ripple the surface. The sun sucked shimmering waves of heat from the water. Now and then, a passing tern would plunge for food, and rise again, and the wavelets from its dive became circles that grew without cease.
>
> The boat sat still in the water, drifting on the tide.

a)   simile – describes something by comparing it with something else, using 'as' or 'like', e.g. 'he ran like a deer'

b)   a short sentence

c)   a sentence with lots of clauses (that include a subject and a verb)

d)   metaphor – describes something by comparing it with something else, using 'is', e.g. 'she is a rock'

e)   powerful verb (action or being word)

f)   powerful adjective (word that describes a noun).

2   Write a sentence describing the effect of each of the techniques you have identified.

Support

You could construct your sentences like this:
* The writer ... to help build up ...
* The writer uses the simile ... to help us imagine ...
* The effect of the adjective ... is ...

Stretch

Add to each of your sentences to explain the effect of the writer's language choices. For example:
'The writer uses a sentence with lots of clauses to help build up the sense of everything being still. It has this effect because the commas make you pause as you are reading, which slows down the pace.'

Now look at the text below, which describes a coral reef. It is an information text, but the writer has chosen words and phrases carefully to bring the description to life.

3 For each of the underlined words and phrases, decide why you think the writer made this choice. To help you, think about the effect the words have on the reader.

e.g. 'rich coral reef' – the adjective 'rich' makes the coral sound special and precious.

There can be few pleasures that compare with snorkelling over a <u>rich coral reef</u>, and in terms of <u>sheer variety and colour</u>, few reefs can match the spectacle <u>fringing the shores of the Red Sea</u>. The surrounding land is a true desert. It is all the more surprising then to stick your head under water and discover a world <u>rich</u> in <u>wonderful</u> designs and <u>bright</u> colours. The water is <u>bath-warm</u> and <u>crystal-clear</u>, and you can float along for hours <u>entranced</u> by an <u>ever-changing</u> <u>kaleidoscope</u> of fish, corals and other invertebrates.

Support

Try to use some of these terms when commenting on the writer's choices:

metaphors	powerful verbs	comparison
adjectives	colour	similes

4 Choose one word or phrase that you think really helps the reader to imagine the scene. Complete the statement below. This will help you to **comment** on the writer's language choices.

The writer has used the phrase _____ to make the reader visualise the scene by _____

Stretch

The writer has used one sentence that is noticeably shorter than the others. Find the sentence and **explain** why the writer wanted to make this sentence different from the others. Then share your explanation with the class.

Apply your learning

Task Working on your own, read the following passage from *Wild Caribbean* by Michael Bright and then answer the questions below to show how well you can now comment on a writer's use of language.

Any mention of the Caribbean is sure to conjure up stunning images of the world's finest beaches, fringed with swaying palms and lapped by an azure sea – a tropical paradise. Here, birds with gaudy feathers and butterflies with see-through wings live in lush, tropical forests filled with orchids and bromeliads; multi-coloured coral reefs bustle with vibrant fishes and menacing reef sharks; white, pink and black sand beaches play host to nesting sea turtles; underground labyrinths of river-filled caverns and seemingly bottomless sinkholes are the secret hideaways for bats, bugs and blind cavefish; prehistoric iguanas and countless lizards scramble across exotic cactuses and thorny scrub; salt ponds and freshwater lakes are graced by coral-coloured flamingos; and the tangled lattice of mangroves is not only home to tree-climbing crabs and roosting seabirds, but also a safe nursery for myriad tiny marine creatures.

GLOSSARY

azure – a light, shade of blue

gaudy – brilliantly coloured

bromeliads – tropical plants

vibrant – brightly coloured

mangroves – tropical trees

myriad – many

1 Explain **how** the writer's choice of words in each of the following phrases suggests that the Caribbean is a 'tropical paradise'.

a) the world's finest beaches

b) birds with gaudy feathers and butterflies with see-through wings live in lush, tropical forests filled with orchids and bromeliads

c) multi-coloured coral reefs bustle with vibrant fishes and menacing reef sharks

d) underground labyrinths of river-filled caverns and seemingly bottomless sinkholes are the secret hideaways for bats, bugs and blind cavefish

2 How does the writer use colour to build up a visual picture of the Caribbean? Find three examples and describe what effect they have.
   e.g. *The writer describes 'white, pink and black sand beaches' which gives the impression that even the sand is colourful and varied.*

3 Reread the long second sentence beginning 'Here, birds ...'

a) How many different details does the writer describe in this sentence?

b) Why do you think the writer has chosen to include all these details in a single sentence? What effect does this create?

4 How do the techniques the writer uses help to create a visual picture of the Caribbean? Copy and complete the following table by picking out your own examples and identifying the techniques used. Then explain how the technique helps us to see what the writer is describing. An example has been completed for you.

Example	Technique	How the technique helps us see what the writer is describing
'the world's <u>finest</u> beaches'	Using a superlative adjective (one ending in -est, meaning 'the most')	It makes us imagine the kind of beaches we see on postcards and on television – the most beautiful beaches in the world, emphasising that they are better than any other.

Assess to Progress

How far have you developed your skills in commenting on a writer's use of language? Ask yourself these questions again:

- Can I identify effective words and phrases from a passage?
- Can I describe the effects these words and phrases create?
- Can I identify particular techniques a writer uses?
- Can I comment on how a writer's language choices affect the reader?

Look back at where you placed yourself on the scale on page 103. Think about where you would place yourself now and why.

1	2	3	4	5	6	7

I find this difficult.   I'm getting there.   I'm good at this.

Choose one of the questions below and answer it in 50 words

1 What was the hardest skill to learn in this unit?

2 What was the most important skill you learnt in this unit?

3 What was the most useful skill you developed in this unit?

4 What skill would you like to learn more about?

Your aunt is thinking of taking a holiday in Corfu. She has heard that it has a great climate, plenty of places of historical interest, and would suit someone in their 50s. However, a friend has told her that it is also full of nightclubs and late night bars. She asks you to find out more about Corfu and you come across the text below from a respected travel organiser.

Read the text so that you can answer the following questions for your aunt:

1   What is there to do on the island that would suit her?

2   Will it be busy and noisy?

3   Which words and phrases does the writer use which make you think this is or isn't the place for her?

CORFU

Beaches

Corfu's beaches are, without a doubt, one of its heavyweight draws. Lassoed by beautiful beaches that all vie for your attention, it's difficult to decide where to lay your sunhat. It really depends on how you like your shores. Cashmere-soft sand or pretty-coloured pebbles? Sweeping curves or secluded coves? Well, don't decide just yet. If you're seeking the Kodak-worthy kind, there are plenty in the running. Pelekas does a good job trying to steal the limelight. A half-moon crescent of sunburnt sand backed by jungle-like hills, it's the perfect picture-postcard. Glyfada is another shimmering hottie. Consistently voted Greece's top beach by the Greeks, it's also a Blue Flag winner. And with honey-coloured sands wide enough to land a 747 on, it's no wonder. If you've got little ones to think about, consider fun-filled Sidari. The shallow waters and beachside eateries with children's menus have made it a firm family favourite.

Sightseeing

Corfu Town

Tangled streets. Shuttered Venetian houses. Rich culture. Corfu Town seduces every which way. Knee-deep in history, this charismatic capital is crammed full of museums. Or ditch the guidebook, and simply get lost in the narrow alleyways of the Venetian old town.

Mount Pantokrátor

Its name means 'the Almighty' and it's no surprise. At 906m, it's Corfu's highest point, so it's worth exploring its slopes. The thrilling views across this lush isle from here are to-die-for. On a cloud-free day you can gaze out as far as Italy. Don't forget your hiking boots. Or your camera for that matter.

Paleokastritsa Monastery

Guarding over the resort of Paleokastritsa below, this much-visited monastery is famous for its jaw-dropping scenic views.

Sidari

As well as its fun-filled reputation, the impressive wave-worn rock formations draw visitors to this pretty resort. Loved-up couples - bring your swimsuits and prepare for a dip.

Achilleion Palace

James Bond fans may recognise this enchanting palace as the set used for the casino in For Your Eyes Only. Built in 1890, it was a retreat for Empress Elizabeth of Austria. Set in verdant gardens, the palace is now packed with fascinating artefacts. It's some serious eye candy.

Korission Lagoon

Gold-dust sands and secluded dunes separate this freshwater lagoon from the glittering Ionian Sea. Exquisite flowers pepper this tranquil spot which remains an unspoilt haven for hundreds of different types of wildlife.

Cassiopeia

Hop over to the mainland and have a poke around some of the sights of ancient Greece. Cassiopeia was without a doubt, one of the most beautiful cities of the ancient world. Visit the Oracle of the Dead and experience the calm of Meteora.

Shopping

If you want to spend an indecent amount of time trying on posh togs or just watch the chic shop, then hit the stylish streets of Corfu Town. Here you'll find elegant leather and handicraft shops as well as boutiques that could well have you blowing your budget.

Nightlife

Every beach in Corfu has its own bar or taverna to keep you refreshed from sun up 'til sun down. Beyond that, it very much depends on what your nightlife cup of tea is. The island does have a reputation for being something of a party island, but if you're looking for a serene escape, don't let this put you off. There are plenty of laid-back lovelies where you can toast the evening without thumping baselines in the background. Wherever you head, make sure you've got a glass of ouzo to hand as you toast your holiday saying 'yamas', which means 'cheers'.

Eating out

The main lip-smacking staple is the Greek food, and it's not to be missed. With all the charming harbours dotted around the island, it'll come as no surprise that fresh-from-the-net fish and seafood is something of a speciality. Step inside any taverna and you'll find it on ice waiting to be picked and cooked to perfection. If the treasures of the deep don't appeal, tuck into Corfiot treats such as 'sofrito', slow-cooked beef in wine, garlic and spices, or 'kreatopita', tender lamb in filo pastry with potatoes, tomatoes and onions. Vegetarians aren't an after-thought here either with delights like 'dolmadakia', vine leaves stuffed with rice, and 'saganaki', deep fried cheese. And don't worry if you'd rather stick with what you know, British-style fare isn't hard to come by.

www.simplytravel.com

Reading AF6
Progress in ... Understanding and responding to ideas, viewpoints and purposes in texts

Reading progress in
es reading progress
se in progress

LEARNING OBJECTIVES

- Identify and understand the main ideas in a text.
- Work out why a text was written (the writer's purpose).
- Identify a writer's viewpoint or opinions in his or her writing.
- Comment on the effect a text has on you as a reader.

Activate your learning

1 Read the text below and think about these questions:

- What are the main ideas?
- Why was it written?
- What do you think the writer wants readers to do?
- How do you feel about what the writer is saying?

Be prepared to share your thoughts in a class discussion.

Why Go Veggie?

The majority of people become vegetarian because they believe it is wrong to kill animals for food and because they are opposed to the cruelty and pain inflicted upon the billions of animals reared. The process of getting a piece of 'meat' onto an individual's dinner plate is the result of much stress and suffering for any animal.

A lot of people find it particularly upsetting to view images or even to read about the average life experience of a farmed animal. It's not pleasant so it can make for a stomach-churning read, but hopefully that is not enough to put everybody off their roast beef or pork chops!

2 Think of three other texts you have read today, e.g. a poster, a sign, a bus ticket or a magazine article. Write down what the three texts were. Then write down why you think the writer wrote it (the purpose of the text); e.g.

It was an advertisement for cars. The writer wanted people to buy a new Mini Cooper.

Assess to Progress

How good are you already at spotting the purpose and viewpoint of different texts? Rate yourself for each skill by deciding which number on the scale below shows your skill level best.

1	2	3	4	5	6	7

I find this difficult.   I'm getting there.   I'm good at this.

- I can identify and understand the main ideas in a text.

  Self-check: Could you pick out the main ideas or points in the *Why Go Veggie* text?

- I can work out the purpose of a text.

  Self-check: Could you identify what the purpose was for the three texts that you read today?

- I can work out what the writer's viewpoint is from a text. Viewpoint means the writer's opinions, thoughts and feelings about what they are writing. A writer can be in favour of something, against something, or neutral.

  Self-check: Think about the text that you have just read. Did you know what the writer's opinion was?

- I can say what effect a text has on me.

  Self-check: Think of a time when reading a particular text, such as an advertisement or news story, changed your feelings about something. Can you explain why it had this effect on you?

Build your skills

This text is a film review from Amazon.co.uk. Follow the skill steps opposite to work out: the main ideas, the text's purpose, the writer's viewpoint and its effect on you as a reader.

Review

While many movie franchises slide as they reach their later instalments, the *Harry Potter* films just keep getting better. The latest, *Harry Potter and the Order of the Phoenix,* is easily the darkest of the series to date, and it's also one of the best. For while it could easily have been little more than a holding film to set up the big encounters to come in the last two instalments of the series, it's to the credit of British director David Yates that the end result is really very good.

It finds Harry coming under suspicion from his wizarding colleagues, who don't believe his claims that the evil Lord Voldemort has returned. *Harry Potter and the Order of the Phoenix* thus finds its title character on the back foot for much of its running time, with a select band who firmly believe his story, and very powerful figures who don't.

Where the movie of *Harry Potter and the Order of the Phoenix* excels though is in its three trump cards. Number one is a far tighter script than we're used to with Potter films, which, combined with trump card number two - the aforementioned David Yates behind the camera – cuts much of the slavish loyalty to the text away in favour of a film with real momentum. The third, and best, card though is the casting of Imelda Staunton as Professor Dolores Umbridge, who simply flies away with every scene she's in. It's a superb performance, and the film is poorer whenever she's not on screen.

GLOSSARY

franchises – permission to film a series
instalments – episodes
trump cards – running cards

Step 1   Work out what the main ideas are

1   Read the whole text. Sum up what each part of it is about. e.g.
The first paragraph tells me that the writer enjoyed watching ...

2   What are the second and third paragraphs about?

Step 2   Work out the text's purpose

Use what you have discovered about the main ideas and ask:

1   What is the writer trying to get readers to do?
To help readers decide whether it is worth ...

2   How do I know I am right? Find a words or phrases from the text that shows this.

Step 3   Work out the writer's viewpoint

1   Look at the first paragraph.
    a)   Does the writer give his or her opinion? What does the writer think and feel about the film in this paragraph?

    b)   Which words or phrases prove you are right?

2   Now focus on the third paragraph. What is the writer's viewpoint here? How can you tell?

Step 4   Think about the effect the text has on you

1   Will the text achieve its purpose and make me do what the writer wanted? Why?
I'd want to see the film because ...

2   Which words or phrases helped you make up your mind?
The words ... made me think ...

Reinforce your skills

Practise using the four skill steps you have just learnt as you work on these activities in groups.

1 Look at the four texts opposite. Work out who wrote each one by reading what the writers have to say about what their **purpose** was when they were writing their text.

1 I'm persuading readers that people will think they have got something fantastic when they own what I'm selling.

3 I am persuading readers to think about how their choice can help others.

2 I want readers to believe that following these instructions is easy and worth the effort.

4 I am giving readers interesting and up to date information.

2 Here are some statements about the writers' **viewpoints**. Decide which are true and which are false. Make notes about which words or phrases in the text helped you to decide.

- The writer of Text A believes that buying OneWater will help people in the developing world.

- The writer of Text B believes that the chocolate fountain is rubbish and no one will want it.

- The writer of Text C is angry that so many people eat unhealthily.

- The viewpoint of Text D is neutral – the writer is telling readers about the research and what the researchers thought.

Stretch

Study Text D again. Pick out the words or phrases that show the researcher's point of view. Explain how they do this.

Support

Use these questions to help you think about your own response to each text.
- Would Text A persuade you to keep buying OneWater? Why?
- Does what the writer of Text B has written about the chocolate fountain make you want to buy it? Why?
- Has the writer of Text C helped you to understand how to eat healthily?
- Are you surprised by what the writer of Text D is telling you?

Text A

Changing lives, one person, one day at a time.

. . . .

Did you know that 1 billion people in the world don't have access to clean water? Or that 2 million people die each year as a result of water related diseases?

When we found this out we wanted to do something to change those figures.

We recognise that it's a massive challenge, but we can change the lives of people – one person, one day at a time.

Simply buy a bottle of OneWater – all our profits, every last drop, go to building unique PlayPump™ water pumping systems overseas which will improve people's lives by providing free, clean water. With your help we can make a difference and that's all we're trying to do.

Text B

LUXURY chocolate fountain. Takes 1kg of chocolate. UK spec and plug. In excellent condition. Very classy centre piece for your dinner party. £20 ono phone daytime: 01726 861096 or 07789 926789

Text C

Easy tips for healthy eating

- Eat at least five portions of fruit and veg each day
- Drink 6–8 glasses of water each day
- Make sure that each day you eat foods from each of these groups: protein, carbohydrates, fats, high fibre foods
- Stop eating before you are full
- Eat slowly, relax and enjoy your meal

Text D

Ice Cream
Fat Stuns Scientists

David Adam, science correspondent

Ice creams and milk shakes bought from parlours that are springing up in shopping centres and cinemas across Britain can contain more fat and calories than burgers and pizzas, US researchers have found.

In some cases a single dessert contains two days' worth of saturated fat, while others are the calorific equivalent of an entire meal. The researchers admit, while they hardly expected to find ice cream a health food, they found the results staggering.

Extend your skills

Sometimes writers express more than one viewpoint and have more than one purpose. Stay alert as you read the whole text and look out for signs that the viewpoint and purpose has changed.

1   Read Jamie Oliver's *Manifesto for School Dinners*. Answer the questions in the boxes about Jamie's **viewpoint**.

a. Jamie's viewpoint here is that a lot of the food children eat is junk. Where else in the text does he show this view?

b. Jamie's view of parents is that they are really important. Find some evidence to prove this.

c. How could you describe Jamie's viewpoint about politicians?

My manifesto for school dinners

For the past couple of years I've been campaigning to ban the junk served in school canteens and get the kids to eat fresh, tasty, nutritious food instead. Without your support for the *Feed Me Better* campaign Tony Blair wouldn't have committed to new school meal standards and to spending £280 million for sorting out the problem.

In my new TV programme, *Return to School Dinners*, we show that <u>parents are a key factor</u>, and that without cooking skills, kitchen facilities and political support on the ground it's going to be very hard to make lasting improvements.

During the course of filming I spoke to the Prime Minister and he promised more and longer term funding for school food. I don't want to sound ungrateful, but the amounts are tiny when you divide it up by all the schools in the country—Nora, for example, only gets £2,000.

This is what I think needs to happen now:

Schools

It's great that kids are going to be taught how to cook at school, but it needs to made a compulsory part of education,

not just a voluntary entitlement. This will require a complete rewrite of the school syllabus to make it appropriate to today's needs, so our kids will learn to understand food, and to cook and shop on a budget—essential life skills.

There's a whole generation of parents out there who were never taught the ease of cooking. This is why the government needs to step in as school is the only place where the kids are going to learn.

Why doesn't the new entitlement cover primary schools too? Kids need to be learning about food right from day one.

Currently, you can pass a food technology course without having to cook. This is totally bonkers! We need to make sure that every teenager leaves school able to cook at least ten healthy dishes as a basis for feeding themselves.

A simple menu of nutritious dishes will give kids the range of basic skills they need to prepare and cook with fresh ingredients, instead of getting their meal from a packet with all of the extra cost, unnecessary processing additives and packaging that goes with it.

d. Jamie has two different views in this paragraph about how well schools are teaching kids about food. What are they?

e. Jamie feels very strongly about children's learning. Which words show how strongly he feels?

GLOSSARY

manifesto – a written statement of aims, beliefs or opinions

committed – promised to become involved in a plan of action

on the ground – at the place where they're needed

Nora – a dinner lady who Jamie Oliver worked with

strategy – plan

entitlement – a right to something

2 Look through the whole text and find two places in his manifesto where Jamie Oliver's **purpose** is:

a) persuading readers

b) explaining something to readers.

3 Which of the statements below do you think best describes Jamie Oliver's **main purpose** in writing this text? Explain why you chose the statement.

I want to persuade readers that a lot more needs to be done if children's eating habits are going to become healthier.

I want to explain to readers how to get children eating more healthily.

Apply your learning

Task Working on your own, read the following text and then answer the questions on the next page. You will achieve a higher level if you can:

- give reasons for your answers
- pick out words or phrases from the text to prove you are right.

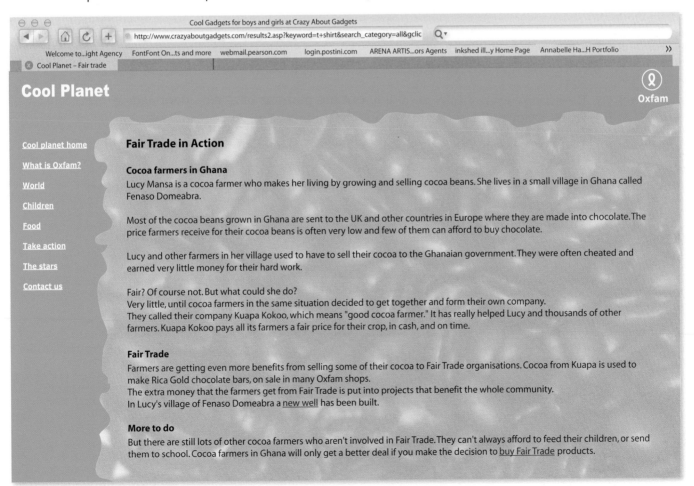

Cool Gadgets for boys and girls at Crazy About Gadgets

http://www.crazyaboutgadgets.com/results2.asp?keyword=t+shirt&search_category=all&gclic

Welcome to...ight Agency   FontFont On...ts and more   webmail.pearson.com   login.postini.com   ARENA ARTIS...ors Agents   inkshed ill...y Home Page   Annabelle Ha...H Portfolio

Cool Planet – Fair trade

Cool Planet

Oxfam

Cool planet home

What is Oxfam?

World

Children

Food

Take action

The stars

Contact us

Fair Trade in Action

Cocoa farmers in Ghana
Lucy Mansa is a cocoa farmer who makes her living by growing and selling cocoa beans. She lives in a small village in Ghana called Fenaso Domeabra.

Most of the cocoa beans grown in Ghana are sent to the UK and other countries in Europe where they are made into chocolate. The price farmers receive for their cocoa beans is often very low and few of them can afford to buy chocolate.

Lucy and other farmers in her village used to have to sell their cocoa to the Ghanaian government. They were often cheated and earned very little money for their hard work.

Fair? Of course not. But what could she do?
Very little, until cocoa farmers in the same situation decided to get together and form their own company. They called their company Kuapa Kokoo, which means "good cocoa farmer." It has really helped Lucy and thousands of other farmers. Kuapa Kokoo pays all its farmers a fair price for their crop, in cash, and on time.

Fair Trade
Farmers are getting even more benefits from selling some of their cocoa to Fair Trade organisations. Cocoa from Kuapa is used to make Rica Gold chocolate bars, on sale in many Oxfam shops.
The extra money that the farmers get from Fair Trade is put into projects that benefit the whole community.
In Lucy's village of Fenaso Domeabra a new well has been built.

More to do
But there are still lots of other cocoa farmers who aren't involved in Fair Trade. They can't always afford to feed their children, or send them to school. Cocoa farmers in Ghana will only get a better deal if you make the decision to buy Fair Trade products.

1 Which of the following statements best describes the main **purpose** of this text? How do you know?

- The writer is persuading the reader to buy Rica gold chocolate bars.

- The writer is explaining why Fair Trade is so important to Ghanaian cocoa farmers.

- The writer is persuading readers that the Ghanaian government really cares about Fair Trade.

- The writer is arguing that everyone should buy Fair Trade goods.

2 Which of these **viewpoints** are present in the text? Pick out phrases that help you to identify the writer's viewpoint.

- It's wrong to rip off people who are very poor.

- Belonging to Fair Trade is not a big deal.

- Our Fair Trade chocolate tastes nice.

- By buying Fair Trade goods you will improve the lives of Ghanaian farmers.

3 Does the writer make you feel that Fair Trade products are worth buying? Refer to the text to give evidence for your answer.

4 How has Fair Trade improved Lucy Mansa's Life?

Assess to Progress

How good are you now at finding out the purpose of a text, identifying a writer's viewpoint and commenting on the effect a text has on you?

1 Look back at the original ratings you gave yourself on page 113. Rate yourself again. Then convince a partner that your ratings should change in the way you have recorded them by giving them evidence based on your work in this unit.

- I can work out the purpose of a text, or what it is trying to achieve.

- I can work out what the writer's viewpoint is from a text.

- I can say what effect a text has on me.

1	2	3	4	5	6	7

I find this difficult.   I'm getting there.   I'm good at this.

2 After closing this book, see if you can note down the four steps you need to follow when you want to work out a text's purpose, the writer's viewpoint and the text's effect on you as a reader.

SKILLS FOR LIFE

Your school is trying to get more speakers to come and talk to pupils about their careers. They think it would help pupils to make informed career choices if they could talk to people about the jobs people do. You are part of a committee that will decide who to invite in to give a talk about their career. You receive this letter and have to make a decision about whether to say yes.

Read the letter and think about:

- what you can tell about the writer

- what you feel about his opinions

- how you react to his writing

- what his motives or purpose might be in volunteering to come into school.

Dear Sam,

I would be very pleased to come and talk to pupils at your school about the real world beyond the school gates. I have views which I think many young people would share. I run a local taxi firm and doing my job you get to know what people are like, what makes them tick. In my opinion the people who are most successful are the ones who don't give up at the first hurdle. They get on without whingeing all the time. Often they were rubbish at school and they have done well because they've learnt about the real world, not the world painted by teachers, many of whom have never done a proper job in their whole life. Driving a taxi takes guts, long hours, honesty and being on time. Most people lack all these qualities and I think it would be a great opportunity for young people at your school to hear about the kind of real-life skills they'll need to develop. I'm happy to come in at any time and speak for an hour or so for free.

Yours faithfully,
Arthur Rodgers

Progress in ... Relating texts to their social and cultural contexts

LEARNING OBJECTIVES

- Explore how ideas and experiences are shown in texts from different cultures and comment on how different readers might respond to these.
- Consider what factors influence writers and understand the ways in which texts reflect the contexts in which they were written.
- Identify similarities and differences between texts from different places and contexts.

Activate your learning

Below are two poems each written by a different poet. These poets come from different countries:

- Grace Nichols was born in the Caribbean country of Guyana in 1950.
- Rudyard Kipling was born in Bombay, India, in 1865 to British parents.

GLOSSARY

mantling – spreading over a surface
plantain – a tropical fruit
replenishing – nourishing

Praise Song for My Mother

You were
water to me
deep and bold and fathoming

You were
moon's eye to me
pull and grained and mantling

You were
sunrise to me
rise and warm and streaming

You were
the fishes red gill to me
the flame trees spread to me
the crab's leg/the fried plantain smell
replenishing replenishing

Go to your wide futures, you said

Mother o' Mine

If I were hanged on the highest hill,
Mother o' mine, O mother o' mine!
I know whose love would follow me still,
Mother o' mine, O mother o' mine!

If I were drowned in the deepest sea,
Mother o' mine, O mother o' mine!
I know whose tears would come down to me,
Mother o' mine, O mother o' mine!

If I were damned of body and soul,
I know whose prayers would make me whole,
Mother o' mine, O mother o' mine!

1   a) Working with a partner, read the poems and decide what each one is about. Discuss the similarities and differences between the two poems. Think about:

● who the poet is speaking to in each poem

● what each writer's attitude is to the person they are speaking to

● the images each poet includes and what these make you think about, e.g. 'If I were drowned in the deepest sea'

● each poet's use of rhyme and repetition.

b) Which poem do you like best? Why?

2   Now see if you can match the poet to their poem. To help you, think about any words or phrases the poet uses that might give you a clue. Compare your choices with another pair and discuss how you reached your decision.

Assess to Progress

1   Think back to the task you've just completed. How good were you at spotting similarities and differences between the poems? With a partner, talk about what you found easy and what you found difficult.

2   Look at the following statements and decide how much you agree or disagree with each of them. Put your answers on the following scale:

1   2   3   4   5

Strongly disagree.   Neither agree   Strongly agree.
                       nor disagree.

● I like to read texts from different places as it is interesting to learn about what life is like in different countries.

● It is important to read the work of writers from a range of backgrounds.

● Reading texts by writers from different cultures helps us to think about our own culture too.

3   Discuss your answers with a partner, explaining your responses to each statement.

In this unit, you will be reading texts from different cultures. At the end of the unit you will have the chance to see whether any of your responses have changed.

Build your skills

The poem opposite is by the Jamaican poet, James Berry. In it he describes the sights, sounds, tastes and smells of his childhood.

1   What do you already know about Jamaica? Talk about your ideas with a partner. If you have access to the internet, research and find out five interesting facts about Jamaica.

2   Now read the poem. What kind of place do you imagine Jamaica to be from this poem? How does this compare with your initial ideas?

3   Are there any words or phrases in the poem that you didn't understand? Using a dictionary, work out the meanings of these words. For example, a 'calabash gourd' is a container made from the fruit of a tropical tree.

4   Which details from the poem help you to create a picture of Jamaica in your mind? Copy and complete the following table, picking out the most striking details that helped to create a sense of place.

Taste	Sound	Smell	Sight

5   If you wrote a poem about the place you grew up in, what details would you include? Brainstorm a list of details using a table like the one above.

6   a) What are the main differences between your list of details and the list from James Berry's poem? Are there any similarities?

    b) Compare your list with a partner and then write a short paragraph explaining how similar or different the place James Berry describes is from the place where you grew up.

Stretch

Pick out details to support the points you make. Here is an example:
James Berry describes a calm and peaceful place where he can hear the 'distant braying of a donkey', but the sounds I hear most days are …
The types of food James Berry describes eating are similar to …

Childhood Tracks

Eating crisp fried fish with plain bread.
Eating sheared ice made into 'snowball'
with syrup in a glass.
Eating young jelly-coconut, mixed
with village-made wet sugar.
Drinking cool water from a calabash gourd
on worked land in the hills.

Smelling a patch of fermenting pineapples
in stillness of hot sunlight.
Smelling mixed whiffs of fish, mango, coffee,
mint, hanging in a market.
Smelling sweaty padding lifted off a donkey's back.

Hearing a nightingale in song
in moonlight and sea-sound.
Hearing the laughter
of barefeet children carrying water.
Hearing a distant braying of a donkey
in a silent hot afternoon.
Hearing palmtrees' leaves rattle
on and on at Christmas time.

Seeing a woman walking in loose floral frock.
Seeing a village workman with bag and machete
under a tree, resting, sweat-washed.
Seeing a tangled land-piece of banana trees
with goats in shades cud-chewing.
Seeing a coil of plaited tobacco
like rope, sold, going in bits.
Seeing children playing in schoolyard
between palm and almond trees.
Seeing children toy-making in a yard
while slants of evening sunlight slowly disappear.
Seeing an evening's dusky hour lit up
by dotted lamplight.
Seeing fishing nets repaired between canoes.

Reinforce your skills

The poem below by Valerie Bloom is also from the Caribbean. It gives another view of childhood in Jamaica and is written in Caribbean Creaole dialect, which is a mixture of West African language and standard English.

Tables

Headmaster a come, mek has'e! Si-down,
Amy! min' yuh bruck Jane collar-bone,
Tom! Tek yuh foot off o' de desk,
Sandra Wallace, mi know yuh vex
But beg yuh get off o'Joseph head.
Tek de lizard off o'Sue neck, Ted!
Sue, mi dear, don bawl so loud,
Thomas, yuh can tell mi why yuh a put de toad
Eena Elivara sandwich bag?
An, Jim, whey yuh a do wid dah bull frog?
Tek i' off mi table! yuh mad?
Mi know yuh chair small, May, but it not dat bad
Day yuh haffe siddung pon de floor!
Jim don' squeeze de frog unda de door,
Put i' through de window – no, no Les!
Mi know yuh hungry, but Mary yeas
Won' full yuh up, so spit it out.
Now go wash de blood outa yuh mout.
Hortense, tek Mary to de nurse.
Nick tek yuh han out o' Mary purse!
Ah wonda who tell all o' yuh
Sey dat dis class-room is a zoo?
Si-down, Headmaster comin' through de door!
"Two ones are two, two twos are four."

1   You may not have understood every word in this poem. Working with a partner, read the poem out loud and try and work out what is happening. Write a paragraph summarising what happens in the poem.

2   How does the impression of childhood you get from this poem contrast with the impression you got from the poem *Childhood Tracks* on page 127? Pick out details and compare these.

Childhood Tracks	What this makes you think	Tables
'Seeing children toy-making in a yard'	This quotation from *Childhood Tracks* gives the impression that children are well-behaved; but the quotation from *Tables* makes them seem noisy and out of control.	'who tell all o' yuh Sey dat dis class-room is a zoo?'

3   Which of these two poems reminds you most of your own childhood? Give reasons for your answer.

Here Valerie Bloom talks about what influences her poetry:

'Music is a big influence. I came from Jamaica. In the Caribbean, the art forms are not separate. You don't just have poetry in one section and music in another, they are all inter-related. And so you would get a poem which has singing and dancing and so on and I draw on that culture when I write, so a lot of my poetry draws on folk songs quite a lot and I use rap in my writing and all those musical forms that I grew up with influence my writing.'

4   Working with a partner, practise different ways of reading the poem aloud to show its musical influences.

Stretch

Looking back at the poem *Tables*, can you pick out any features that show how music has influenced Valerie Bloom's writing? Think about:
*   the rhyme scheme of the poem
*   the vocabulary used.

Extend your skills

Now read this poem by the black British poet Benjamin Zephaniah.

1   What is this poem about? Think back to the poems you read in the Activate your learning section.

2   Write a paragraph comparing this poem with either *Mother o'Mine* or *Praise Song for my Mother*. In your paragraph, make sure you comment on:

●   what each writer's attitude is to the person they are speaking to

●   the images each poet includes and what these make you think about, e.g. 'she have big muscles and she very very strong'

●   each poet's use of rhyme and repetition

●   the mood of the poem, e.g. is it humorous or sombre?

I LOVE ME MUDDER ...

I lover me mudder and me mudder love me
we come so far from over de sea,
we heard dat de streets were paved with gold
sometime it hot sometime it cold
I love me mudder and me mudder love me
we try fe live in harmony
you might know her as Valerie
but to me she is my mummy.

She shouts at me daddy so loud some time
she don't smoke weed she don't drink wine
she always do the best she can
she work damn hard down ina England,
She's always singing some kind of song
she have big muscles and she very very strong.
she likes pussy cats an she love cashew nuts
she don't bother with no ifs and buts.

I love me mudder and me mudder love me
we come so far from over de sea
we heard dat de streets were paved with gold
sometime it hot sometime it cold,
I love her and she love me too
and dis is a love I know is true
me and my mudder we love you too.

Stretch

Benjamin Zephaniah was brought up in Birmingham, but his poetry is influenced by the music and poetry of Jamaica. What similarities are there between Valerie Bloom's poem *Tables* and *I love me mudder*? Think about:
•   the rhyme scheme
•   the use of dialect words such as 'dis' and 'mudder'.

Apply your learning

The poem below is about the Caribbean immigrants who arrived in Britain in the 1940s and 50s at the invitation of the British government who needed more workers. The first wave of immigrants arrived on a ship from Jamaica called *Empire Windrush* and the people who came to Britain from the Caribbean at this time were called the 'Windrush' generation.

Windrush Child by John Agard

Behind you
Windrush child
palm trees wave goodbye

above you
Windrush child
seabirds asking why

around you
Windrush child
blue water rolling by

beside you
Windrush child
your Windrush mum and dad

think of storytime yard
and mango mornings

and new beginnings
doors closing and opening

will things turn out right?
At least the ship will arrive
in midsummer light

and you Windrush child
think of grandmother
telling you don't forget to write

and with one last hug
walk good walk good
and the sea's wheel carries on spinning

and from that place England
you tell her in a letter
of your Windrush adventure

stepping in a big ship
not knowing how long the journey
or that you're stepping into history

bringing your Caribbean eye
to another horizon
grandmother's words your shining
beacon

learning how to fly
the kite of your dreams
in an English sky

Windrush child
walking good walking good
in a mind-opening
meeting of snow and sun

Task **1** Which of the following words would you use to describe the mood and feelings of the author of this poem? Give reasons for your choice. You could also choose your own words if you want.

| hopeful | excited | happy | sad | worried | confused | angry | nervous |

2   a) What impression do you get about what life was like in Jamaica from the poem?

   b) Pick out some details from the poem that help to give an impression of life in Jamaica. Explain why you think the writer has included these.

3   What impression do you get about life in England from the poem? What details show how life in England is different from life in Jamaica?

4   Heading for a new life in a country you have never been to seems like a massive step into the unknown. Looking back at the poem, pick out details that help you to understand why people came from Jamaica to Britain at this time.

5   Think about the other poems you have read in this unit.

   a) How do the details about Jamaica included in the poems *Childhood Tracks* and *Tables* help you to understand how somebody might feel about moving away from their home in Jamaica?

   b) In *I Love me Mudder* the poet says 'we come so far from over de sea/we heard dat de streets were paved with gold'. What do you think this is referring to now you have read *Windrush Child*?

   c) Of the poems you have read, which is your favourite? Write a paragraph explaining your choice.

Assess to Progress

Look again at the following statements and decide how much you agree or disagree with them. Put your answers on the following scale:

| 1 | 2 | 3 | 4 | 5 |

Strongly disagree. Neither agree Strongly agree.
nor disagree.

- I like to read texts from different places as it is interesting to learn about what life is like in different countries.

- It is important to read writers from a range of backgrounds.

- Reading texts by writers from different cultures helps us to think about our own culture too.

Have your ratings changed at all? Discuss your answers with a partner.

SKILLS FOR LIFE

Your school is arranging an educational trip to the Caribbean. Here is some information about the Caribbean countries that will be visited and the activities planned:

> The Dominican Republic is a picture-postcard Caribbean paradise with white sand beaches, impressive mountains and rainforests full of amazing wildlife. Organised trips led by local guides and teachers will help visiting pupils understand the varied geography of the region at first-hand. Sporting opportunities are also a fixture of this school visit to the Caribbean, with Barbados providing pupils with opportunities to practise their cricket, beach football and snorkelling skills and learn from local sporting heroes. Jamaica provides the musical heartbeat of the Caribbean with a strong reggae culture that is brought to life for pupils through live music events and workshops where they can share in the musical culture with local pupils.

Using the information about the trip given above, prepare a short statement explaining why you should be chosen to go on the trip. In your statement you should comment on:

- why you want to take part in the trip

- how taking part will help you in different school subjects

- which part of the trip you would most look forward to and why.

Reading

Assessing your Progress

- Understand and select information from a text.
- Use evidence in a text to infer and deduce meanings.
- Comment on the way a text is structured.
- Use the right technical terms to explain how writers create setting, character and mood through their choice of words and sentence structures.
- Comment on the effects of a text on the reader.

Working through this unit will give you the opportunity to show the progress you have made in your reading skills. You will read an extract from a ghost story and have the chance to show your skills in identifying how writers imply meaning and how their words and sentences create setting, character and mood.

Activate your learning

1   What are the typical ingredients of a ghost story? Working in pairs, think about ghost stories you have read or seen on film or TV. Make a list of the key features they have in common. Here are a couple of ideas to get you started:

- Some unexplained events – these might be scary, unexpected or ...

- A ghost: there are different types of ghosts in different stories, for example ...

2   Compare your list with another pair. Which ideas did you both have? Were there any ideas that you could add to your own list?

Build your skills

You are going to read an extract from a ghost story. Before you start, think about the reading strategies that might be helpful to you as you read.

1   From the strategies listed below:

   a) Identify the ones that you use frequently and explain how they help you to make meaning from texts.

   b) Choose one that you sould use more often. Explain how and why you would use it.

READING STRATEGIES

- **Questioning:** Ask questions about the events, characters or the way the story has been written.

- **Predicting:** Use clues in the text to work out what might happen next.

- **Visualising:** Have a picture of the people and places in the story you are reading.

- **Reading backwards and forwards:** Reread to check details and scan ahead to check how the story develops.

- **Inferring and deducing:** 'Read between the lines' to work out what the writer is suggesting.

You may sometimes come across a word that you don't understand. When this happens, you could try these techniques, known as 'reading searchlights'.

READING SEARCHLIGHTS

- Sounding out a word. This is called **phonics** where you break the word down into separate sounds so you can hear the word.

- Recognising a word. This is called **graphical knowledge** where you look at the shape of the word and groups of letters that you can identify.

- Using your **grammatical knowledge** to think about what kind of word would make sense. Read around the word to work out the context and what sort of word it is. Then think of an alternative word that would do the same job and make sense.

- Reading on (and looking back) to search for clues. This is called using **contextual knowledge** where you reread a few sentences and scan ahead to understand the context.

2   Think about a time when you have used reading searchlights. You might use the first two quite regularly, but you should try to use the last two when you encounter words you don't understand.

To help you understand what 'tangible' means, use your **knowledge of grammar and context** to work out what kind of word would make sense here.

3 Here are the first four paragraphs from the ghost story, *The Red Room* by H.G. Wells. As you read them, try to use the reading strategies and searchlights indicated in the boxes around the text:

'I can assure you,' said I, 'that it will take a very tangible ghost to frighten me.' And I stood up before the fire with my glass in my hand.

Predicting. Do you think he will see a ghost? What clues in the text makes you think this?

Use your **grammatical knowledge** to work out the purpose of the word 'askance' and reread the sentence to understand the **context**.

'It is your own choosing,' said the man with the withered arm, and glanced at me askance.

'Eight-and-twenty years,' said I, 'I have lived, and never a ghost have I seen as yet.'

Inferring and deducing. The narrator tells us he hasn't ever seen a ghost. What does this tell us about the narrator and the events in this house?

Visualising. Try to see the scene in your head, like a video. Describe to your partner the details can you see.

The old woman sat staring hard into the fire, her pale eyes wide open. 'Ay,' she broke in; 'and eight-and-twenty years you have lived and never seen the likes of this house, I reckon. There's a many things to see, when one's still but eight-and-twenty.' She swayed her head slowly from side to side. 'A many things to see and sorrow for.'

Questioning. Think about what you have read. What questions do you still have about the characters and plot?

4 Now read the next part of the extract from *The Red Room*, remembering to use as many reading strategies as you can.

I half suspected the old people were trying to enhance the spiritual terrors of their house by their droning insistence. I put down my empty glass on the table and looked about the room and caught a glimpse of myself, abbreviated and broadened to an impossible sturdiness, in the queer old mirror at the end of the room. 'Well,' I said, 'if I see anything tonight I shall be so much the wiser. For I come to business with an open mind.'

'It's your own choosing,' said the man with the withered arm once more.

I heard the sound of a stick and a shambling step on the flags in the passage outside, and the door creaked on its hinges as a second old man entered, more bent, more wrinkled, more aged even than the first. He supported himself by a single crutch, his eyes were covered by a shade, and his lower lip, half averted, hung pale and pink from his decaying yellow teeth. He made straight for an arm-chair on the opposite side of the table, sat down clumsily, and began to cough. The man with the withered arm gave this new-comer a short glance of positive dislike; the old woman took no notice of his arrival, but remained with her eyes fixed steadily on the fire.

'I said – it's your own choosing,' said the man with the withered arm when the coughing had ceased for a while.

'It's my own choosing,' I answered.

The man with the shade became aware of my presence for the first time, and threw his head back for a moment and sideways, to see me. I caught a momentary glimpse of his eyes, small and bright and inflamed. Then he began to cough and splutter again.

5 Talk to a partner about the reading searchlights and reading strategies you used. Find out what different strategies your partner used. Which ones did you find most useful?

Assess to Progress

How well did you use the reading strategies?

1   Choose one of the reading strategies and explain how it helped you to make meaning from the text by completing one of the following sentences.

- Questioning helped me understand the text by ...

- When I predicted what might happen next, it helped by ...

- Visualising the characters and events was useful because ...

- Reading backwards and forwards helped me to ...

- I used inference and deduction. This was useful because ...

2   Identify one difficulty you might have when reading another extract from this story. Which reading strategy would help you to overcome this difficulty?

Reinforce your learning

Look at this question about the text you have just read:

Let's work out what this question is asking us to do:

> The answer must focus on these characters. Are there different things to say about each of them?

> This is asking you to explain the writer's techniques. It is important to think about how the characters speak as well as what they look like.

How do the three old people create a ghostly atmosphere?

> This is the mood or feeling in the room.

A good answer will try to make a few different points and support these with details from the text. Using the wording from the question to organise your answer can also help.

1. Reread the description at the bottom of the previous page of what a good answer will do. Which parts of this do you think you can do well and which will you need to work on?

2. Now read these two pupils' responses to the question. Working in pairs, decide which you think gives the best answer to the question and explain why.

SAM'S ANSWER

The old people look horrible. One has a withered arm and another one's got yellow teeth. They make you feel yuk! You wouldn't want to stay in a house with them. I don't like them at all. They are trying to frighten the man in the story. The man with the withered arm keeps going on about "It's your own choosing".

DAVID'S ANSWER

The writer creates a ghostly atmosphere because the two old men seem to belong in a horror story. One has a withered arm and the other has a lot of disgusting things about him:

- decaying yellow teeth
- his lower lip
- his eyes
- his coughing and spluttering.

Also the way the old woman speaks makes you think something horrible is going to happen: 'many things to see and sorrow for'.

Support

Which of these comments best describe Sam's answer? Which best describe David's?

- It is a personal response.
- This response shows that what the old people say is just as important as their appearance in creating the atmosphere.
- There are some relevant references to the text.
- The pupil uses the key words from the question to organise the answer.
- The response does not include clear comments on the writer's techniques.
- The references to the appearance of the old men are more precise and clearly linked to the first main point.

Now decide which response you think gives the best answer to the question.

Extend your learning

You are now going to read the rest of the extract from the story.

1   First, summarise what we know from the story so far. Make a list like this:

   ● It is a ghost story.

   ● There are three old people ...

2   What do you think might happen in the next section of the story? Explain your prediction, making sure you base it on evidence from the story so far.

3   Now read the final extract from the story, using some of the reading strategies you practised earlier.

'If,' said I, 'you will show me to this haunted room of yours, I will make myself comfortable there.'

The old man with the cough jerked his head back so suddenly that it startled me, and shot another glance of his red eyes at me from under the shade; but no one answered me. I waited a minute, glancing from one to the other.

'If,' I said a little louder, 'if you will show me to this haunted room of yours, I will relieve you from the task of entertaining me.'

'There's a candle on the slab outside the door,' said the man with the withered arm, looking at my feet as he addressed me. 'But if you go to the red room tonight –'

'This night of all nights!' said the old woman. 'You go alone.'

'Very well,' I answered. 'And which way do I go?'

'You go along the passage for a bit,' said he, 'until you come to a door, and through that is a spiral staircase, and half way up that is a landing and another door covered with baize. Go through that and down the long corridor to the end, and the red room is on your left up the steps.'

'Have I got that right?' said the man with the shade, looking at me again for the third time, with that queer, unnatural tilting of the face.

'This night of all nights!' said the old woman.

'It is what I came for,' I said, and moved towards the door. As I did so, the old man with the shade rose and staggered round the table, so as to be closer to the others and to the fire. At the door I turned and looked at them, and saw they were all close together, dark against the firelight, staring at me over their shoulders, with an intent expression on their ancient faces.

'Good-night,' I said, setting the door open.

'It's your own choosing,' said the man with the withered arm.

I left the door wide open until the candle was well alight, and then I shut them in and walked down the chilly, echoing passage.

4   Look at the following question:

Reread the paragraph that begins "It is what I came for'. How do we know that the old people are frightened?

We need to use inference and deduction to answer this question. Reread the paragraph, using the following guidance to help you to work out your answer:

● Firstly, look at what the old man does – he moves closer to the others. From this, we might infer that he feels he doesn't want to be alone. What else could we infer from his action? For example, why might he want to be closer to the fire?

● What about the rest of the old people? They are 'all close together'. They are 'staring at me over their shoulders' and have 'an intent expression' on their faces. How does each of these details suggest they are frightened?

5   Now look at Jo's answer to the question:

The man with the shade moves so that he is close to the others. The old people seem to be huddled close together as if they feel safer that way.

In pairs, give Jo some feedback. Explain what is good about the answer and any ways that it could be improved.

> ## Stretch
>
> Rewrite the answer to show the improvements that you want to make. You could include some direct quotations and make additional inferences.

6   What other reading strategies do you think you used when you were reading this extract? Choose another paragraph. Working with a partner, explain the reading strategy you used and how it helped you to understand the text.

Progress task

Working on your own, complete all of the questions that follow to show how your reading skills have developed. These questions are all about the extracts from *The Red Room* that you have read in this unit.

You should spend about five minutes on each question. If you get stuck, go on to the next question and return to that question later.

Questions 1 to 5 are about the final extract from the story on page 140.

1   The old man tells the young man how to get to the red room. Read again the paragraph that begins "You go along the passage for a bit', in which the old man gives him directions.

Look at the map below, which is based on what the old man said. Some of the labels on the map are missing. Write down what should go on the missing labels.

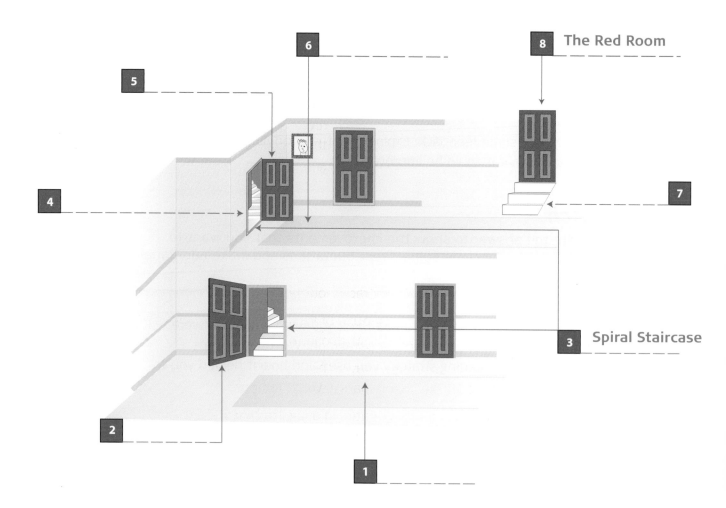

8   The Red Room

3   Spiral Staircase

2 Find one piece of information which tells us that the young man will need some light to find his way to the red room. Find and copy a quotation which proves this.

Information:

Quotation:

---

3 How do we know that the young man is bored with the old people and wants to get on with the ghost hunting? Write your answer in a paragraph.

4 Why do you think the old people don't offer to go to the red room with the young man? Write your answer in a paragraph.

5 Find two examples of words or groups of words which help to create a ghostly atmosphere. Copy and complete the table below to explain how you think they do this. One example has been provided to help you.

Examples of words or groups of words	How they create a ghostly atmosphere
1 'dark against the firelight'	These words make it seem as though the room is very dark and the only light is from the fire. Dark rooms always seem creepy and spooky.
2	
3	

Questions 6 and 7 are about all of the extracts you have read.

6 The writer repeats some words and groups of words at different points in the story. This helps to build up the suspense.

One example is when the old woman says 'This night of all nights' and then repeats it just before the young man leaves the room.

Find some more words which are repeated in a similar way and explain how successfully you think they build suspense. You may base your answers on the whole extract from the story or just on the last section.

The writer repeats the words ...

I think this builds the suspense well because ...

---

7 Here are three pupils' responses to the story. Select the one you think would most please the writer and explain why you think this. Write a paragraph for your answer.

A The story was quite creepy because I didn't know what was going to happen to the man in the red room. I wouldn't have spent the night there.

B I thought the story was really funny. The old people made me laugh.

C I felt upset when I read the story because it was so sad. I felt sorry for the young man.

> The statement I have chosen is A / B / C.
> I think the writer would be most pleased with this response because ...

Assess to Progress

1 Which questions did you feel most confident about answering? Which questions did you feel less confident about?

2 Swap work with a partner. Look at their answers to questions 3 and 4. These were **inference** questions. Which of the following statements do you think best describes the quality of their answers?

- Straightforward comments show understanding of the literal meanings of the text and may be based on **speculation**.

- Answers make inferences based on some textual evidence but may repeat the content or not be developed.

- Answers develop explanations which are based on textual evidence. These answers might have a point, evidence, and an explanation.

What do you think they could do to improve the answers they have given? Explain your advice.

3 Look at your own answer to question 5. This asked about how the writer used words to create atmosphere. Select a statement from the list below that best describes the quality of the answer:

- Identifies one or two appropriate words or phrases but does not make relevant comments on the writer's choice. They may have used words from the example answer to model their own response.

- Identifies words or phrases and makes straightforward comments about the intended effect.

- Identifies words and phrases and shows some awareness of the effect of the writer's language choices.

What do you think you could do to improve your responses?

Progress in ...
Writing

Writing AF1
Progress in ... Generating ideas, planning and drafting

Activate your learning

1   You have five minutes to plan an advert for a holiday that would appeal to teenagers. First, list the ways you can make your advert interesting for readers and have a real impact on them. Think about the details you could include and any techniques you would use.

2   Sketch out a plan of the layout for your advert, showing where any pictures, text or headings would go. (You don't need to create a masterpiece – labelled boxes will do.)

3   Decide what your headline will be.

4   Compare your ideas with the rest of your class:

   - How many people came up with very similar ideas for the holiday?

   - Whose ideas for ways to lay out or write the advertisement were similar?

   - Whose ideas were original? Discuss how they came up with them.

Assess to Progress

How well can you generate ideas and plan your writing? How good are you at developing your ideas into an imaginative and interesting piece of writing? Rate yourself for each of the skills below by deciding which number on the scale shows your skill level best.

| 1 | 2 | 3 | 4 | 5 | 6 | 7 |

I find this difficult.   I'm getting there.   I'm good at this.

- I can generate lots of ideas.

  Self-check: Did you come up with lots of ideas for the holiday and how to present it in the advert or was it a struggle to think of even one?

- I can work out which of my ideas is likely to be different from most other people's, and find ways to improve it.

  Self-check: When you had an idea for the advert, did you think of ways to improve it or did you just write it down in the way that it popped into your head?

- I can use different methods of planning a text.

  Self-check: How many different ways can you use to plan a text? e.g. making a list of headings. How easy do you find it to choose the most helpful planning format?

- I know the conventions of different text types and how to use and vary them.

  Self-check: Give yourself a minute to recall what ingredients are needed for: a) an advertisement, b) a set of instructions, c) a story, d) an argument.

- I can write in an original, imaginative and interesting way.

  Self-check: When you are writing, do you use a wide vocabulary, making sure you choose the best words and images? Are you confident about using different techniques to help make your writing more effective?

- I can use editing and proofreading skills to make improvements to my writing.

  Self-check: When you finish the first draft of a piece of writing, do you always read it through and look for ways to improve it?

Build your skills

If you want to write well, it is important to spend time planning. To practise this, think about how you would write some instructions to help people your age try a new activity at the weekend. Answering the following questions will help you to come up with good ideas and plan your writing effectively.

1   **What is my purpose in writing this text?**
    To write some instructions on …

2   **Who are my readers?**
    People my age, so what I choose will have to appeal to boys/girls/both aged …

3   **What type of text am I writing? What features should it have?**
    Instructions have a heading telling readers …
    They use numbered …
    Sentences that begin with … verbs.

4   **How can I think of an idea that will be interesting for my readers?**
    a) Think about what you have to write and spend a few minutes brainstorming a list of possibilities. Don't stop to think about whether they are any good at this stage.
    How about swimming, a skateboarding competition, setting up a sumo wrestling party …

    b) Judge your ideas – which will work well? Which ideas will be different from other people's?
    Swimming **X**   Skateboarding **X**   Basketball marathon – maybe
    Sumo wrestling party ✔

5   **How can I make a useful plan?**
    There are lots of different ways of planning a piece of writing, including spider diagrams, tables, flow charts and lists. Some examples are provided opposite.
    a) Choose the best way to plan the type of text you are writing, e.g. a chart might be best for a carefully organised argument. Which kind of plan will suit your instructions?

    b) Fill in the content of your plan by asking yourself lots of questions: Where? When? Who? What? Why? Which? How?

Support

When completing your plan, write notes not whole sentences. Jot down details. Number the points in the order you will write about them.

Chart with columns and rows

Instructions for setting up a sumo wrestling event with your friends	
Introduction	What is sumo wrestling – why try it?
What do you need to do before the big day?	Invites, suits, rules, sumo area in which to fight, referee, salt, camera or video
Where can you get the equipment?	
On the day: what are the rules for sumo wrestling?	
Keeping everyone safe and having fun	
Clearing up afterwards	
Conclusion	What to do with all those amazing photos ...

Flow chart

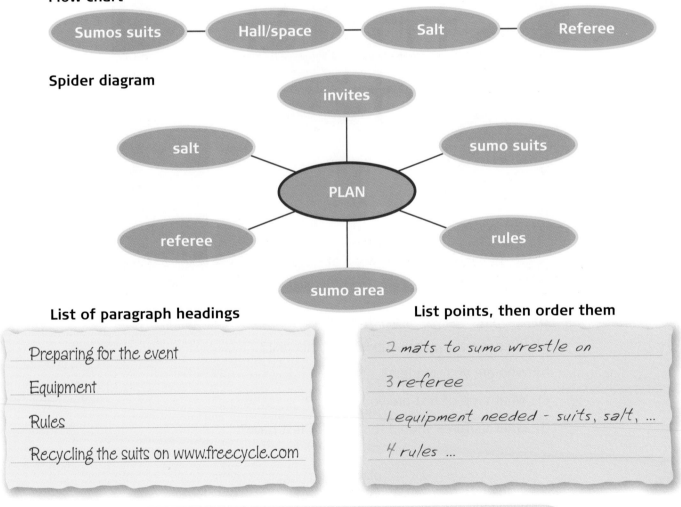

Sumos suits — Hall/space — Salt — Referee

Spider diagram

invites

salt

sumo suits

PLAN

referee

rules

sumo area

List of paragraph headings

Preparing for the event

Equipment

Rules

Recycling the suits on www.freecycle.com

List points, then order them

2 mats to sumo wrestle on

3 referee

1 equipment needed - suits, salt, ...

4 rules ...

Stretch

Which type of planning format would you use for a) a story, b) a discussion? Why?

Reinforce your skills

You are now going to plan and write a piece of travel writing about a journey. You can choose any journey you like: it can be about something very familiar, such as your journey to school, or more exotic – have you visited a volcano or walked through a bustling market on holiday? To make travel writing interesting for readers you need to write about your thoughts, feelings and experiences in a lively and engaging way.

1   Work in a group and answer these questions:

  a) What is your purpose in writing this text?

  b) Who are your readers?

  c) What type of text are you writing?

  d) What features should this type of text have?

2 Working on your own, decide what journey you are going to write about. Spend a few minutes picturing yourself making the journey to try to remember in detail what you saw, heard, smelt, thought and felt. Jot down notes about the experience.

3 Working with a partner, help each other to think through what you can tell readers about the journey. Take it in turn to be A and B.

Person A: Picture making the journey in your head. Describe it to your partner and jot down notes about:

- the different stages in the journey, e.g. landmarks, where you buy something

- what your senses notice, e.g. sounds, smells

- what the atmosphere is like, e.g. happy, bustling, dreary, cold

- any people you meet

- the events that happen during your journey

- how you feel, and what your thoughts are about the things you notice.

Person B: Listen to your partner talking about the journey. Prompt them to think about interesting details by asking them questions about what they noticed, e.g. What was the weather like? How rainy?

4 Turn your notes into a detailed plan, using a chart, a list of paragraph topics or a flow chart. Think carefully about:

- how your text will start. How will you make sure it grabs readers' attention?

- the order in which you will describe things. Number your plan to help you.

- how your piece of writing will end. How will you make it feel rounded off?

Extend your skills

When you have planned your text, you then need to make sure you write it in an imaginative and interesting way.

1   Working in a group, read writer and TV presenter Kate Humble's piece of travel writing about her journey on the Ffestiniog railway. It is aimed at readers who have never been on this journey. Answer the questions in the boxes around the text.

> Which of Kate's senses noticed these details? Where in the text has she written about what she heard?

> Kate has used this word to show her opinions and feelings. Which other words and phrases do this? What impression do they give you of the journey?

> How does this image help you to picture the railway?

> What image is used here to help you picture the train? How does this make the writing more interesting and vivid?

> How does Kate's choice of words help readers to picture and hear the way the steam train moves? Hint: say the words out loud and listen out for any changes in rhythm.

Boarding the train I was hit by a <u>warm fug and that certain smell of old fabric and excited bodies</u>. I sat down on a blue threadbare seat elaborately adorned with the Railway Ffestiniog insignia and fringed with fraying cotton. I gazed at the <u>wonderful view from</u> my window as we left Porthmadog behind us. Over the cob the train picked up speed clouds of steam floating past the windows the smell of smoke, coal dust and warm metal added to the excitement as I felt like I was travelling back in time. The landscape was so varied with views of the sea, houses and stations. We approached Minffordd station and there were people on the platform anticipating our arrival. <u>It looked exactly like a giant version of a model railway</u>, the paintwork immaculate. And spectators waved as we journeyed up the mountain. We stopped at Tan-y-Bwlch where the train is filled up with water. <u>The engine bubbled and spluttered and took on water as if it had a really dry throat</u>. With a whistle and a lurch we were off again, <u>a series of jolts, squeaks and rattles</u> until the train eventually settled in to that comforting steady chug.

You are now going to use some of Kate's writing techniques in your own piece of travel writing that you started to plan in the previous section.

2   a) Working with a partner, take it in turns to talk for a minute about what can you see, hear and smell at the start of your journey.

    b) On your own, draft two sentences which give details that will help your reader really picture the scene. Use describing words to tell readers what your senses noticed.

3   How did you feel about making your journey? Was there anything that made you feel excited, amused or sad, for example? Write two sentences describing what made you feel that way.

4   Look back at the way Kate used images in her writing. Choose two things you saw on your journey. What can you compare them with so that your reader will be able to picture them vividly? Write sentences that include these images.

5   Look at the way Kate used the sounds and rhythms of words to give impact to her description of the way the train moved. Make a list of words that describe the movements and sounds of the way you travelled on your journey. Then write a sentence using some of these words to describe how you travelled along.

6   a) Share the sentences you have written with your partner and work together to improve them. You might need to use a thesaurus to find more powerful words. Try to add extra details to help your reader imagine the scene.

    b) Using the sentences you have drafted already, complete the first draft of your piece of travel writing describing your journey. Remember to make it imaginative and interesting for your readers.

7   When you have completed your first draft you will need to check it through carefully to see where and how you can improve it. Use the questions below to help you do this:

●   Does your opening grab readers' attention? How could you improve it, e.g. by creating a vivid atmosphere, using a question or giving a surprising fact.

●   Are there any places where you could make your description more powerful, e.g. by adding images or feelings? Think about the ways you could help readers to picture the journey more clearly.

●   Does every sentence make sense? Can you spot any spelling, grammar or punctuation mistakes?

8   Write your final draft, including all the improvements you have made. Remember to give it a final proofread to spot any spelling, grammar or punctuation mistakes you can correct.

Apply your learning

Task Working on your own, write a description of a day spent at the beach.

Spend the first ten minutes jotting down some notes as you:

- brainstorm ideas for what to write about
- develop your best idea into one that will work well for your description
- plan your descriptive writing.

You should also decide on the viewpoint you will use to tell the story – through whose eyes will the reader experience the story?

Make sure you think carefully about the words you choose, use of imagery and other techniques you can use to help you write an imaginative and interesting description.

Remember to use your proofreading and editing skills to make improvements to your writing.

Assess to Progress

How good are you now at each of these skills? Rate yourself for each skill by deciding which number on the scale below shows your skill level best.

| 1 | 2 | 3 | 4 | 5 | 6 | 7 |

I find this difficult. I'm getting there. I'm good at this.

- I can generate lots of ideas.
- I can use different methods of planning a text.
- I know the conventions of different text types and how to use and vary them.
- I can write in an original, imaginative and interesting way.
- I check and improve my writing and I proofread my final draft carefully.

You are helping to edit the school magazine. It is aimed at parents, students and governors and is supposed to give an interesting account of what is going on in the school. It is published at the end of each term.

Your friend Jo has submitted an article about a school visit to France. You know that all the students who went on the visit had a good time, but that isn't clear from Jo's report.

1 Read the opening of Jo's article and make notes on how it could be improved:

   ▪ Which sentences and words would you change or cut?

   ▪ What would you change to make it more interesting?

   ▪ Are there enough details of people, places, textures and colours? Are there too many details in places?

2 Decide how to improve the article and write a new draft to make it more interesting. Then, write a short email to Jo explaining the changes you have made and the reasons for these.

> I was really looking forward to going to France because I hadn't been to France before. I have been learning French for two years but had never had chance to try speaking it and I didn't really know anything about life in France except what I had read in the textbook we use. When we were told we were going to stay in a place called Annecy I hadn't heard of it before so I looked it up and found that it was in the French Alps. It was therefore going to be a very long journey by coach.
>
> When the day came to set off I was quite nervous and I hadn't really slept much the night before because I was afraid that I would sleep through the alarm or forget to take something important. I probably only had about four hours sleep. We had to be at school at 6am and my mum drove me there. My friends were already there, except Kerry who's usually late and was this time, and it was very dark and very cold and everyone seemed a bit nervous to be honest. Mr Nettleton called out our names and said we could put our bags in the bus and get on. I realised then that I'd forgotten my iPod and got really down about it.

Progress in ... Writing texts to fit context, purpose and audience

LEARNING OBJECTIVES

- Use different levels of formality in texts according to context, purpose and audience.
- Draw on your knowledge of different forms of writing to plan your writing and develop ideas to fit a specific task.

Activate your learning

1 Work with a partner to decide what is wrong with each of the four pieces of writing below.

Dearest Laura,
I would be honoured by your company this Saturday at the Trafford Centre. It would please me very much indeed if you would accompany me on my shopping excursion in pursuit of spending all my hard-earned pocket money on items of apparel.
Yours truly
Faye

Options Reply Back

A'right ladies and germs?

I'm not lovin' the shaved eyebrows look that's goin round school at the mo. Get it sorted or else!

Love
The head teacher

Dear Mrs Roberts,

Thomas has been off school for three days suffering from a severe case of streptococcal pharyngitis which showed itself clearly as red pustules on his pharynx. He also had extremely marked tonsillar exudates, which responded well to treatment, although his cervical lymph nodes are still somewhat enlarged. If you could see to it that he does not over-exert himself, I would be much obliged.

Mrs Rudd

Frosted Krazy Wheaty-flakes

Filled with dangerous chemicals, a load of added stuff you don't need and some vitamins what you don't understand.

2   How should each writer have written the text to get their message across effectively?

3   Choose one of the texts. Rewrite it so that it is appropriate for the audience and purpose of that text.

Assess to Progress

How well can you write with the task, audience and purpose in mind already? How easy do you find it to choose the right level of formality?

Think about the different types of writing that you do as well as the activity you have just completed. Then decide how highly you should rate yourself for each of the skills below. Be ready to prove that your scores are realistic.

1	2	3	4	5	6	7

I find this difficult.   I'm getting there.   I'm good at this.

- I can draw on what I know about different types of texts when planning my writing and thinking of ideas.

- I know what features to use when I am asked to write different types of texts.

  e.g. I know what layout features to use in a newspaper article.

- I think about the purpose of the task before writing.

  e.g. I ask myself whether I am writing to give information, or advice, or to persuade someone to do something.

- I think about who will be reading my writing and try to make changes for different readers.

  e.g. I write using simpler language if I am writing for young children.

- I can choose whether to use formal or informal language depending on the task.

  e.g. I don't use slang if I am writing a letter to someone I don't know.

Build your skills

Read this web page about the martial art, capoeira. After you have read it, use the steps on the next page to explore the text.

Capoeira!

A martial art where you don't make contact? Where you kick and move, but nobody gets hurt? Almost seems like it wouldn't be as much fun as its big brothers, judo and karate, yet to watch capoeira is to watch art in action, and is to see the human body undertake movement as you've never seen it before!

Jugo

The word 'jugo' means game, which is what capoeira is supposed to be. In the past, when the Brazilian slaves were forbidden from practising martial arts, they made their martial arts into a game to fool the slave-owners. It's played in a rodo, which is a circle where others watch and sing. Music is a key part of the jugo – but more about that later.

The moves

There are three main moves you might notice when watching the capoeiristas (that's the people taking part in it) although they can be tricky to spot because of the speed of it.

The first type of moves are attack–defence moves. The one thing you will notice about these is that one capoeirista will attack by kicking, whilst their opponent will move away either by moving back or to the side. They may even go for the trick move and attack as well. When watching, it seems so fast and chaotic that you are just waiting for a foot to make contact: but that's the skill, they never do!

Step 1   Think about the purpose and audience of the writing

1   The **purpose** of this text is to inform readers. What is it telling the reader about? What information is given in the first section?

2   Which of these **audiences** do you think the writer is aiming at?

- older people who like sport
- young people who like sport
- young people who want to know how to do something
- older people who want to know how to do something.

Point to evidence in the text to explain your choice.

Step 2   Think about the structure and form of the writing

1   The writer uses a main heading and some sub-headings. Why do you think this is?

2   The sections are quite short. Why has the writer used this structure? Hint: think of the audience, as well as where the text can be found.

3   Informative texts link information so the reader can follow the ideas clearly. Do you think the writer of this text has done this?

4   In an information text, it is usual to begin with some general information about a topic, then go into detail. Does the writer do that here? Point to evidence in the text to explain your view.

Step 3   Think about the language and style of the writing

1   Although this an information text, the writer has tried to make the sport sound exciting. Even the heading has an exclamation mark. Where else does the writer use language to make capoeira sound exciting?

2   The writer begins with some questions. How effective is this technique?

3   Like most information texts, this is written in the present tense, e.g. 'It's played in a rodo'. Why do you think writers use the present tense for this type of writing?

4   Information texts often also explain things. Which words has the writer explained?

5   Powerful words and phrases are used to paint a colourful picture of the sport, and to grab the reader's interest. Pick out two examples and explain why they are effective.

6   The writer has not used a very formal style. For example, the contraction 'don't' is used. Why do you think this style is appropriate?

Reinforce your skills

When you write, you need to think about how formal or informal your language needs to be for the type of text you are producing and your audience. For example, an encyclopaedia entry about France suitable for anyone would use more formal language than a postcard to a friend.

1   Look at this list of language features:

- specialist vocabulary

- shortened pronouns and verbs, e.g. I'll, you'd

- informal greetings

- slang words, e.g. telly, dosh.

   a) Decide which of the following texts and audiences it would be most appropriate to use each of the different features in. Discuss your answers with a partner.

   - A text message to a friend.

   - A science report for your teacher.

   - An article in a magazine for teenagers.

   b) Look back at the texts on page 154. Explain why the formality of each piece of writing is inappropriate for its audience.

When you write you need to be clear about the **purpose** of your writing, e.g. is it to inform, to persuade or to instruct? Some texts have more than one purpose (e.g. the capoeira text both informs and entertains). It is important to make sure the features you use suit the purpose.

2   a) In pairs, read the extracts opposite and match them to the purpose and the typical features of that type of writing.

   b) Discuss your answers with another pair, picking out words and phrases that helped you make your decision.

> ## Support
>
> Choose one writing purpose and look at the list of typical language features used in this type of writing. Now read each text in turn and try to find examples of any of these features. To help you, think about any other texts you have read that have the same purpose (to instruct, for example) and decide which of these texts most remind you of this type of text.

Peel the plums by placing them in boiling water for a minute until the skins are easy to pull from the flesh. When you are removing the plums from the water, ensure all the water has been poured away. Then add the plums to the pan with two tablespoons of caster sugar.

Without your support, our dogs' home could not survive. Your donations mean thousands of animals have a safe, warm and caring environment where they can recover from any number of tragedies that they have seen in their short lives. Please give generously.

Being the new kid on the block can be a traumatic experience, but there are plenty of things you can do if you move school. Spend some time watching the different groups around the school and think about where you'd feel most comfortable. Look for others who have the same hobbies and interests as you.

MUMMIES

Many different societies used mummification to preserve the dead, but the most famous mummies are those found in the Egyptian tombs. Mummies are simply preserved bodies that do not rot because they have been treated in some way. Most mummies, though, are created by natural causes, where drying winds, extreme cold or extreme heat preserves the soft tissue of the bodies.

To instruct

Set out in time order, often in list form
Simple and clear language
Uses commands, e.g. 'Take ...'

To advise

Main points first, detail later
Often includes technical words
Often written in present tense
May be organised in sections, with headings

To persuade

A series of points aimed at getting you to do something
Personal language – the reader is addressed directly
Powerful words to grab your interest
Powerful images to make you feel things

To inform

Addresses the reader directly
Shows the reader that they understand their situation
Often uses a conversational tone
A series of points

3   Dale has written a short informative article for his school magazine about his hobby of keeping snakes.

a) Read the article and discuss the comments below it with a partner. How fair are they?

keeping snakes

I have been raising snakes since I was seven years old. My first snake was 'Flakes' who is a corn snake. My dad bought him for me from a reptile breeder. I have to keep him in a secure cage because he's very good at getting out and then my mum goes mad! Corn snakes do bite but they aren't poisonous. Flakes is about five feet long now and he has to have a big cage so he has plenty of spaces to hide in. Corn snakes can live about twenty years in captivity, but they don't live as long as that in the wild. They come from Florida mainly so they need to be kept in a warm room. I have a heat pad under one end of the vivarium so that he can go to keep warm there if it gets a bit cold. Sometimes he likes to lie in his water bowl though if he gets hot. We feed our snakes with dead mice which we buy frozen from the pet shop. We have to defrost these before we give them to our snakes. We only need to feed them twice a month otherwise they get fat! They also shed their skin.

- The personal information is good and gives it a human touch, but the other information is a bit dull.
- The headline and order of information isn't very appealing. It just has one long paragraph and the information isn't really in any kind of an order.
- The information is clear, but it isn't very interesting or exciting to read. There isn't anything here to make it sound really unusual or interesting as a hobby.
- Dale hasn't really used any layout features to help make this look like an article for a school magazine.

b) Pick out the informative words and phrases that Dale has used. How could you add words to them, or change them, to make them sound more interesting?

c) With your partner, rewrite the article to respond to the comments. Show that you can choose the right style to interest the audience and use an appropriate layout.

Extend your skills

When you are writing, it is important to use words and phrases that are suitable for the audience and purpose of your text. For example:

● Should you address the reader directly?

● Should you use formal or informal language?

1   Working with a partner, read the short examples in the table below and think about the language used in each one. How appropriate is it for the audience? Does the style of the language help to achieve the purpose of the text?

e.g. 'Come to Farnworth because it's Da Business!' is too informal – the guide wouldn't want to put people off. It should be something like, 'Come to Farnworth because everything you need is here!'

Text	Example
A guidebook for your local town	Come to Farnworth because it's Da Business!
A recipe	Just throw a load of peas into a blender and give them a whizz.
A set of instructions on how to put up shelves	Don't be an idiot – don't forget to nail the panel to the back!
An internet guide on how to improve the security of your computer	If at all possible, you may wish to purchase an additional add-on package from your local software retailer.
A brochure advertising holidays in Spain	We have 200 apartments. There is a big pool in the middle of the complex. There are lots of families here.
A persuasive letter from a charity asking for your donations	Give us some of your money. You don't need it half as much as these kids do. They have nothing while you sit about eating too much and getting fat!
Information from a local sports centre about football coaching in the summer holidays	Your child may be interested in improving his or her cardio-vascular health and fitness, or improving their co-ordination and motivation.

2 In pairs, pick an activity or hobby that you enjoy, and make a list of its main elements. For example:

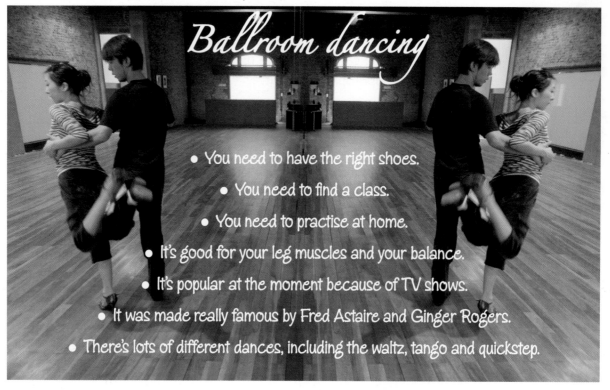

Ballroom dancing

- You need to have the right shoes.
- You need to find a class.
- You need to practise at home.
- It's good for your leg muscles and your balance.
- It's popular at the moment because of TV shows.
- It was made really famous by Fred Astaire and Ginger Rogers.
- There's lots of different dances, including the waltz, tango and quickstep.

a) One of you should write a paragraph for an **informative** leaflet about the benefits of your hobby or activity. It should be written for parents who have children interested in taking up your hobby.

b) The other person should write a short section for a website to **persuade** others to take part in the activity. It should be aimed at teenagers who are using the internet to research the hobby before they decide whether to take it up.

Support

Use the following questions to help you:
- What is my **purpose** for writing?
- What type of **text** am I producing?
- What **features** should it include?
- How **formal** should my writing be in order to make it appropriate for the audience?

c) When you have completed your writing, ask your partner to identify five words or phrases that they think you could change or improve to make the style more appropriate for the purpose and audience.

d) Make the changes. In the margin, write notes to explain what changes or additions you made, and why.

Look at the example opposite, where Dalvir explains what he has added into his paragraph.

I added a rhetorical question to get the reader thinking.

I added some superlative adjectives here to emphasise how hard it is and why people do it.

I remembered that some people wouldn't know what aerodynamics means, so I explained it.

<u>When you think of sport, which is the fastest, the most flash and the most exciting</u>? Formula 1 racing might seem to be just a lot of fast cars driving around a track, <u>but it's a sport of precision and concentration</u>. Formula 1 racing is one of the most popular sports and its drivers are some of our <u>biggest</u> celebrities. It is the <u>most difficult</u> and the <u>most rewarding</u> motor sport. <u>Aerodynamics, technology, and driver skill are the three main factors for success. Aerodynamics is the science of keeping the car on the track and making its shape cut through the wind, making the car go as fast as it can</u>. You also might not think that racing drivers have to be fit, but race car drivers are among the fittest sportsmen on the earth.

I changed the second sentence from 'it's a sport where you have to take care and think hard' to 'it's a sport of precision and concentration' to make it sound more interesting and more difficult.

4 a) Why do you think Dalvir chose to write without using 'I'? What difference is there between:

Formula 1 racing is one of the most popular sports and its drivers are some of our biggest celebrities.	Formula 1 is my favourite sport and the drivers are my heroes.

b) What else do you think Dalvir did to make sure his writing was appropriate to a wide audience?

Stretch

Dalvir has quite often used 'you' in his work. How else could Dalvir speak to the reader? Formal writing often avoids using first and second person pronouns, such as 'I' and 'you'. Why do you think it isn't always appropriate to use these in this type of writing?

Apply your learning

Task Working on your own, complete the task below. You need to show that you can write with a clear purpose, thinking about your audience and using an appropriate level of formality.

> Your school librarian has asked you to produce a piece of informative writing about one of your hobbies to display in the school library as part of a showcase on hobbies and activities. They would like to use these to help people select books and magazines on particular hobbies to get more pupils using the library.

1   Before you start to write, think about:

● the purpose of your writing – what features should you use?

● the audience for your writing – how formal or informal does your language need to be?

● the details you could include and how you should present these

● choosing the right tense for your writing.

2   When you have completed your first draft, reread it and make changes so that your writing is even more suitable for your audience and purpose.

Assess to Progress

How well can you write with readers and purpose in mind now? Think about the writing that you have completed in this unit. Look back at the ratings you gave yourself at the beginning of the unit and decide whether any of them should change. Be ready to prove that your scores are realistic.

1	2	3	4	5	6	7

I find this difficult.   I'm getting there.   I'm good at this.

● I can draw on what I know about different types of texts when planning my writing and thinking of ideas.

● I know what features to use when I am asked to write different types of texts.

● I think about the purpose of the task before writing.

● I think about who will be reading my writing and try to make changes for different readers.

● I can choose whether to use formal or informal language depending on the task.

Your friend, Lucy, is standing in the school election for the Student Council. The role will involve organising social events and raising money for charity. Candidates have to write 100 words about themselves, which will be read aloud in assembly.

Lucy's draft begins like this:

> Hiya! My name's Lucy Tennant and I'd love to be your new student rep!

1   Lucy isn't sure whether she should change her text to make it:

-   more formal, by getting rid of 'Hiya!' altogether or changing it to 'Hello' and changing 'rep' to 'representative'

-   more informal, keeping 'Hiya!' and cutting her surname to make it more friendly.

What would you advise her to do? Why?

2   a) Using the information below, write the next three sentences of Lucy's statement:

-   She has been a sports leader for netball.

-   She is keen to represent the views of all students.

-   She has ideas for improving the school.

b) With a partner, discuss how you have written the text to make it appropriate for the audience and purpose, picking out words and phrases to help you explain.

LEARNING OBJECTIVES

- Recognise some different ways in which whole texts are structured and use clear openings and endings in your own writing.
- Organise ideas in a logical sequence, using different techniques to help you do this.
- Shaping the overall organisation of the texts you write to communicate ideas clearly and effectively.

Activate your learning

Working with a partner, decide where in a story you would expect to find each of these phrases: at the beginning, middle or end? Explain your decision.

The first one has been done for you:

a) Veronica stared back suspiciously, and Shameem gulped.

Answer: I think this is from the middle because it doesn't introduce the characters – it assumes we know them. It seems like they are in the middle of something.

b) Suddenly a man appeared ...

c) Once upon a time ...

d) She looked tired, filthy and hungry ...

e) And they lived happily ever after.

f) "No!" Dad barked back. "Absolutely not!"

g) The screaming drifted over the hills and she knew it would never end.

h) Darkness fell.

i) The next day I couldn't find it anywhere.

j) I remember this time at my primary school when ...

k) It was a place I'd never see again.

l) It was a perfectly peaceful afternoon at home when ...

Assess to Progress

How well do you organise your writing to make sure you express your ideas clearly?

Copy the grid below and tick the relevant box next to each skill. Be as honest as you can. This will help you to set targets for your learning in this unit.

If you need help, look at a recent piece of informative writing you have done (in English or any other lesson).

I can ...	Easily	Sometimes	Not very often
Use paragraphs to organise my ideas logically and create links between these.			
Create effective openings and endings when I write fiction texts such as stories.			
Create effective openings and endings when I write non-fiction texts such as reports and essays.			

If you have ticked 'not very often' or 'sometimes' for any of the skills, concentrate on improving these skills as you work through the unit.

Build your skills

Most stories follow this pattern or structure:

1 They start off in a normal situation or state of balance.

2 Something happens to disturb the balance (a change usually meaning trouble).

3 A new situation or balance is established at the end.

This structure doesn't just work for fiction: many true-life narratives, news stories and documentaries are organised in the same way. It helps the reader to follow events through from the beginning to the end, and to feel involved in the story.

Here are examples of how a fairy tale and a feature film fit the pattern.

	Cinderella	*Star Wars IV: A New Hope*
1. Beginning situation or state of **balance**	Cinderella is lonely, unhappy and bullied by her ugly sisters.	Luke Skywalker is an orphan living with his aunt and uncle and working on their farm on the Planet Tattooine.
2. Something happens to **disturb the balance**	Cinderella is sent to the ball by her fairy godmother and the prince falls in love with her.	Luke's aunt and uncle are killed and he goes with Ben Kenobi to rescue Princess Leia from the Empire.
3. **A new balance** is established at the end	Cinderella is happily married to the prince.	Luke destroys the Death Star and is awarded a medal of Valour by the Rebel Alliance.

1   Think of another story. Complete a copy of the table above for this story. You could use another film, book or cartoon, e.g. *Harry Potter and the Deathly Hallows*, *Spiderman* or an episode of *The Simpsons*.

Writers use paragraphs to organise their writing. **Paragraphs** group material on the same topic or idea together. A new paragraph is used whenever there is some sort of change, for example:

● Time – a movement forward or backwards in time.

● Focus – when a different thing or character is being described.

● Place – when the action shifts from one place to another.

● Viewpoint – when you show a different point of view.

● Speaker – a new paragraph starting each time there is a new speaker.

2   Read the newspaper article on the next page. Answer the question in the boxes to explore how the text is structured.

REVEALED: TITANIC WAS DOOMED BEFORE IT SET SAIL

by Jasper Copping, *Sunday Telegraph*

The *Titanic* faced disaster from the moment it set sail, experts now believe. Research suggests that, even if the ocean liner had not struck an iceberg during its maiden voyage, structural weaknesses made it vulnerable to any stormy sea. The flaws, uncovered by researchers who found, filmed and analysed previously undiscovered portions of the *Titanic's* keel, also reduced the length of time the vessel remained afloat after hitting the iceberg on April 14, 1912 – scuppering the chances of rescue boats sent to the scene arriving in time and thus condemning hundreds of passengers and crew stranded on board to death.

To date, the received wisdom has been that after striking the iceberg, water flooded into the ship. The weight of the water in the bow forced the vessel's stern to rise until, when it reached an angle of 45 degrees, the ship snapped in half and sank. It is that version of events that was depicted in the 1997 Oscar-winning film *Titanic*, starring Leonardo DiCaprio and Kate Winslet.

However, the findings of the new research project, a collaboration between the History Channel and Lone Wolf Documentary Group, an American film company, suggest that the Titanic broke in half when its stern had reached an angle of just 10 degrees - a scenario that could have occurred in heavy seas during any severe storm, never mind in the aftermath of hitting an iceberg.

The opening sentence of this paragraph tells us what the story is going to be about.

The rest of the paragraph gives us the details of why the Titanic was doomed. It expands on the opening sentence by adding detail.

The opening sentence of the next paragraph also tells us something important – what?

How does the rest of the paragraph support this sentence?

The writer begins a new paragraph here because it is a new topic. What is the new topic?

How does the ending link back to the opening sentence?

Stretch

The article uses the three-part structure in an unusual way:
- Researchers analysed newly discovered pieces of wreckage;
- It is commonly thought that the Titanic sank when it reached an angle of 45 degrees and snapped after hitting an iceberg;
- It is now thought that it could have sunk after snapping at an angle of just 10 degrees.

Why might news stories play with the story structure and order of events?

What other texts might reverse the order in this way?

GLOSSARY

aftermath – period of time after a major event
collaboration – joint effort
condemning – sentencing
keel – main structural element of a ship
maiden voyage – first journey
scuppering – ruining

Reinforce your skills

Below is an eyewitness account of the sinking of the *Titanic*. However, there are no paragraphs in the text and you need to decide where they should go, using the guidelines on page 168. Remember, the purpose of the text is to describe clearly what happened. This means you need to use paragraphs to help the reader follow the sequence of events.

1   Working in a pair, identify where you would start each new paragraph and the reason why.

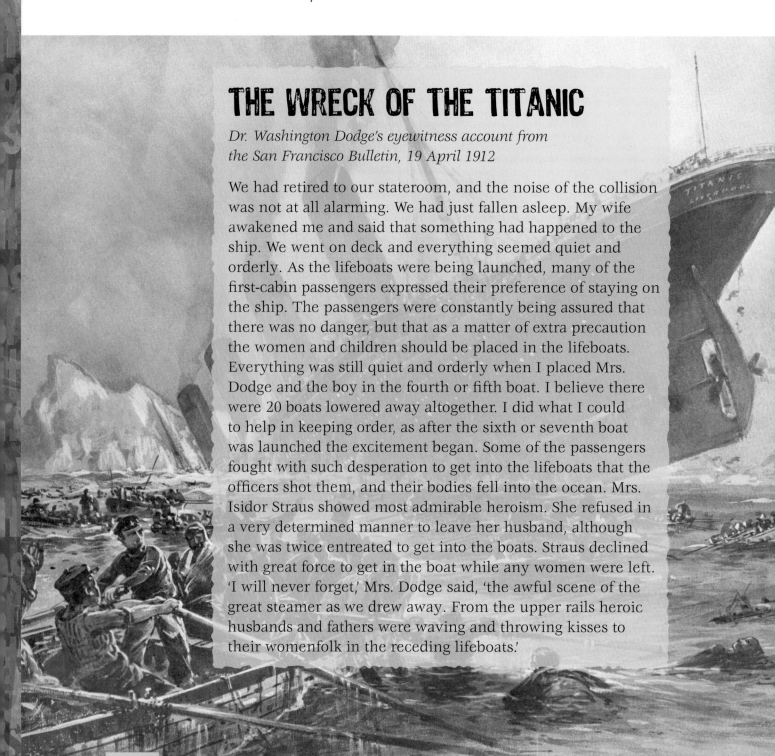

THE WRECK OF THE TITANIC

Dr. Washington Dodge's eyewitness account from the San Francisco Bulletin, 19 April 1912

We had retired to our stateroom, and the noise of the collision was not at all alarming. We had just fallen asleep. My wife awakened me and said that something had happened to the ship. We went on deck and everything seemed quiet and orderly. As the lifeboats were being launched, many of the first-cabin passengers expressed their preference of staying on the ship. The passengers were constantly being assured that there was no danger, but that as a matter of extra precaution the women and children should be placed in the lifeboats. Everything was still quiet and orderly when I placed Mrs. Dodge and the boy in the fourth or fifth boat. I believe there were 20 boats lowered away altogether. I did what I could to help in keeping order, as after the sixth or seventh boat was launched the excitement began. Some of the passengers fought with such desperation to get into the lifeboats that the officers shot them, and their bodies fell into the ocean. Mrs. Isidor Straus showed most admirable heroism. She refused in a very determined manner to leave her husband, although she was twice entreated to get into the boats. Straus declined with great force to get in the boat while any women were left. 'I will never forget,' Mrs. Dodge said, 'the awful scene of the great steamer as we drew away. From the upper rails heroic husbands and fathers were waving and throwing kisses to their womenfolk in the receding lifeboats.'

Extend your skills

As well as knowing when to use paragraphs, it is important to be able to sequence your paragraphs in a logical order, and to show how ideas are connected.

1 a) On the next page is an article from the charity Islamic Relief, about a seven-year-old survivor of the 2004 Boxing Day tsunami in south-east Asia. The paragraphs have been muddled up. Your task, working in a small group, is to decide on the right order. You should:

- look for links between the paragraphs, e.g. paragraph f ends with the words 'Nola clung on to whatever she could find.' Which paragraph starts with a sentence that links back to this?

- think about which paragraphs would be the most effective opening and ending.

b) Record the correct sequence of paragraphs by drawing a diagram like the one below.

c) Compare your paragraph choices with another pair. Did you paragraph the account in the same way or were there differences?

> ## Support
> Follow the three-stage structure you read about on page 169.
> Identify:
> - the situation at the beginning, which is normal and everyday
> - the paragraphs that describe dramatic changes to this situation
> - the new situation at the end.

2 Annotate the diagram to show what the link is between each paragraph?

3 How does the ending of the article link back to the opening paragraph.

4 Now copy and complete these sentences to explain what you found out about the structure of the text.

- The article starts with paragraph ... This is a good opening because ...

- The situation is changed dramatically in paragraphs ... In these paragraphs the writer describes ...

- The article ends with a paragraph ... I know this because ...

ORPHANED BY THE TSUNAMI

a 'I found myself holding on to a piece of wood', says Nola. She doesn't know how long she clung to the driftwood, but it was a long time before a stranger rescued her.

b Seven-year-old Nola Presti Arisma used to live with her mother, father and two younger sisters in Banda Aceh before the tsunami struck. On the 26th of December 2004, Nola was watching television with her family when a great earthquake shook their home, its epicentre only 255 km to the south.

c There are an estimated 400,000 people living in camps who, like Nola, lost everything in the disaster. Islamic Relief is helping them with food, water and sanitation.

d Sadly, the rest of Nola's family died in the disaster, and she now lives with her grandmother in one of the several camps in Banda Aceh for people who lost their homes. She attends school in the mornings and then visits the graveyard with her grandmother to pray for her family. In the afternoon she goes to the mosque to learn the Qur'an.

e When asked about her life in the camp Nola answers bravely, 'I like it here; I have lots of new friends and a good teacher too. I want to be a doctor, and my teacher says I am very clever.'

f In panic they ran out of the house. Cries of 'water, water is coming' filled the streets as a vast wall of water surged through their home. Nola's mother held her in her arms and struggled to hold on against the waves until she couldn't anymore. Taken from her mother's arms by the sea, Nola clung on to whatever she could find.

Apply your learning

Task Now you are going to bring your skills together to write an eyewitness account of a disaster. This account can be of a real or made-up situation, but in your account you should:

● create an effective opening that captures the reader's attention

● use paragraphs effectively to move the narrative on, linking ideas and events in a logical sequence

● create an effective ending – this could link back to the opening.

Use the plan below to help you generate ideas and think about how to structure your account.

Generating ideas
First decide what sort of disaster you are going to write about: Flood? Shipwreck? Avalanche? Tornado? Plague of frogs?

Opening:
Setting the scene
What was going on just before the disaster?
How are you going to make it seem normal and realistic for your reader?

Middle:
Describing the events that change everything
How did the disaster happen?
What was the sequence of events?
How did you and others react? What dramatic details can you give?

Ending:
Describing the new situation
How has the situation changed from the beginning?
How does the narrator feel about what happened?
How has it changed him/her and what has s/he learned?

Assess to Progress

Working with a partner, you are going to evaluate each other's eyewitness accounts.

1   Team up with a partner for a peer evaluation of your eyewitness account. Look at each other's work and answer these questions before giving feedback:

   ● Think about the organisation of the whole text – does it have a clear beginning, middle and ending?

   ● Think about the paragraphing – has the writer organised their ideas well?

   ● Do new paragraphs start when you would expect them to?

2   In this unit you have learnt about some different ways to structure your writing. How good are you now at each of these skills?

   ● Recognising some of the different ways texts can be structured and how openings and endings can be created

   ● Organising your ideas in a logical sequence in your writing

   ● Making sure your overall organisation of the text helps make your ideas clear.

Look at the chart which you filled in at the start of this unit. Try it again and see what you have improved on. Use the work that you have done in this unit to prove to your partner that your new ratings are the correct ones.

3   Now complete the sentences below:

   I have improved the way I organise my writing as I now can …

   I still need to improve …

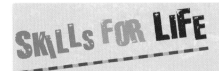

SKILLS FOR LIFE

You are on work experience at a plumbing company. They ask you to work on a leaflet. The leaflet is designed to give readers information about the company and to persuade them to use their services.

The problem is that the current draft is very disorganised and confusing.

> We do all kinds of plumbing jobs, from installing new appliances to sorting out leaks and overflows.
>
> Established in 1982, we have a superb reputation for a job well done.
>
> We are a small local company with a team of four professional plumbers.
>
> We guarantee our work: if you're not happy we're not happy and we'll refund your money.
>
> For more information call us on 01788244566.
>
> A good plumber is hard to find. Fuller & Fuller offer you the best service and reliability.
>
> We do jobs like these:
>
> Installing dishwashers and washing machines
>
> Mending leaks
>
> Putting in new shower units and baths
>
> Responding to sudden pipe bursts

How would you improve it?

1 Decide on a catchy headline or slogan.

2 Put the text in the best order.

3 Set it out with an appropriate image so that it becomes an eye-catching leaflet.

Progress in ... Using paragraphs to make ideas clear

LEARNING OBJECTIVES ⭐

- Organise writing into appropriate paragraphs to make your ideas clear.
- Use connectives (linking words and phrases) to join paragraphs effectively.
- Link sentences within paragraphs.

Activate your learning

Here is the opening of a short story that has been chopped into single sentences and the sentences have been jumbled up.

A 'Mum,' I finally decided to whisper, 'Mum'.

B I turned my head and there, in the middle of the sofa between my mum and me was a very large – and I mean disgustingly large – spider.

C In fact, I still am.

D Sure enough, after a few seconds the spider scurried down the middle of the sofa towards my mum.

E It sat there and didn't move, but I knew that it would soon.

F 'Why didn't you tell me?' she shouted.

G It was something that moved – I didn't know what.

H When I was little, I was quite afraid of spiders.

I I wasn't sure whether to mention it to my mum or just run across the room.

J So I edged off the sofa and waited and watched to see what the spider did.

K One evening I was sitting with Mum watching the telly when I noticed something out of the corner of my eye.

L 'Shut up,' she said: 'I'm enjoying this'.

M The problem was that we lived in quite an old house and it was full of spiders.

N She shrieked and jumped up.

Working with a partner, complete the following tasks:

1   Decide what the text is about.

2   Put the sentences in the order that you think is correct.

3   Decide how many paragraphs you think the story should have and where each new paragraph should start.

Compare your answers with those of other people in your class.

Assess to Progress

How well can you use paragraphs already?

Rate yourself for each of the skills below by placing yourself on the scale.

1	2	3	4	5	6	7

I find this difficult.   I'm getting there.   I'm good at this.

● I can organise different texts into paragraphs.

   Self-check: You're given any text at random, all in one long paragraph. It might be a story, an article, a recipe or a report. Can you sort it into paragraphs that will help the reader to follow it?

● I can link sentences within paragraphs.

   Self-check: You've written a draft response to a text you are studying in English, but your teacher says that you jump from one idea to another. Can you reorganise it so that sentences within paragraphs link with each other better?

● I can use connectives to link paragraphs.

   Self-check: When you look at the first and last sentence of most of your paragraphs, do they often contain a connective which helps connect one paragraph to the next?

Build your skills

When you write non-fiction texts, such as reports, there are usually four main reasons to start a new paragraph:

- Change of topic
- Change of time
- To make a new point within a topic
- Change of viewpoint.

1 Read this extract about Queen Elizabeth I from a history textbook. It is written in short paragraphs. Decide which of the reasons above explains why the writer has started each new paragraph.

Elizabeth I

In 2002 British television viewers placed Elizabeth I seventh in the list of great Britons. Why?

Elizabeth I was born in 1533 and was a powerful and sometimes ruthless figure. She is sometimes referred to as Good Queen Bess and her reign is seen as something of a golden age. She remained in power until her death in 1603.

The later stages of her rule were a period when drama flourished. Shakespeare became the most famous writer of his day and with his company performed before the Queen.

Nowadays not all historians accept the idea that this was a glorious moment in history. Expert Mike Foley says: 'Forget all the stuff about a golden age. This was a period when people were brutally treated – imprisoned and even killed if they did not agree with the "official" views of the state, and a time when the English were overseas invading other countries and stealing their valuables.'

Other historians think Foley overstates the case ...

When writing fiction texts, such as novels and short stories, there are five main reasons for starting a new paragraph:

- Change of speaker.

- Change of time.

- Change of place.

- Change of viewpoint.

- For a special effect, e.g. to create suspense or increase the pace.

2 Read the following extract from the novel *Millions* by Frank Cottrell Boyce. In the novel, Britain is changing from using the pound to using the Euro and trains are taking all the old pound notes to a secret location to be burnt. The novel is narrated by Damian who has an older brother called Anthony.

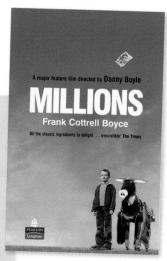

> Anthony said goodbye to the old pound nearly every day. On the way home from school, he used to run like mad to the middle of the footbridge, then wait there till a train went roaring by beneath us. Then he'd wave and yell until it was out of sight, just like the Railway Children, shouting, 'Goodbye! Goodbye, old pounds!'
>
> He made it sound like every single ten-pound note was a personal friend. Sometimes you'd think he was going to cry. 'Just think,' he'd say, '500-odd years of history, up in smoke.'
>
> Other times, he'd seem quite happy about it. 'Just think,' he'd say, 'come Christmas we'll be able to spend the same money from Galway to Greece.'
>
> Every night before we went to bed, the three of us dropped any small coins we had into a big whisky bottle at the foot of the stairs. On the way to bed, Anthony would nearly weep as he dropped his five pees in. On the way to breakfast, he'd stroke the bottle happily and say 'Amazing how fast it mounts up.'
>
> Personally, I think, so what? Money's just a thing and things change. That's what I've found. One minute something's really there, right next to you, and you can cuddle up to it. The next it just melts away, like a Malteser.

a) For each paragraph, decide which of the reasons above best explains why the writer has started a new paragraph.

b) Compare your answers with your partner and see how far you agree on the reasons.

Reinforce your skills

Organising your writing doesn't just mean knowing when to start a new paragraph. It is also important to link your ideas within paragraphs. Pete has been asked to write a paragraph describing his favourite childhood toy. Read what he has written.

> I remember when I was a child. I was about six. I had an Action Man. The Action Man had fake hair. The fake hair was a funny grey colour. The grey hair had a strange texture. The texture was soft. The texture was also a bit bristly. The Action Man was my favourite toy for a long time.

Pete's paragraph contains lots of repetition. Writers can avoid repetition by:

- using pronouns to refer back to nouns they have used, e.g. they, this, that, he, she, we.

- using connectives to link back, e.g. then, also, similarly, however, next.

- making sentences more interesting and complex, by adding relative clauses (that begin with 'that', 'which', 'who') and adding phrases (that begin with 'on', 'in', 'through', 'under').

Now look at how Pete has rewritten the paragraph to make it less repetitive.

> I remember when I was a child of about six. I had an Action Man with fake hair that was a funny grey colour and which had a strange texture. It was soft but also a bit bristly. He was my favourite toy for a long time.

- He has used pronouns ('it', 'he',) to refer back to earlier nouns ('hair', 'Action Man').

- He has used connectives ('and', 'but') to extend sentences, linking ideas together.

- He has added relative clauses (beginning 'that' and 'which') to make sentences more interesting and complex.

1 The text below has been written for a museum guidebook about dinosaurs. You have been asked to improve the text and make it more interesting to read. Use the techniques you have learnt for organising paragraphs and linking sentences within paragraphs.

Before you rewrite the text, think about:

- which sentences to keep

- which sentences to delete

- which sentences to link together to make the text more interesting

- where you need to start new paragraphs.

Dinosaurs

Dinosaurs lived on the earth a long time ago.

Dinosaurs are all dead now.

The last dinosaurs died about 65 million years ago.

Dinosaurs were the biggest land animals to ever live upon the earth.

There were hundreds of different kinds of dinosaurs.

We know what dinosaurs looked like from their skeletons. Scientists have studied the bones.

Scientists believe that birds may be direct descendants of some dinosaurs.

The 'Dinosaur Age' is divided into three time periods.

The three time periods are the Triassic, Jurassic and Cretaceous periods.

The first dinosaurs lived near the end of the Triassic period.

One of the first dinosaurs was the Herrerasaurus.

The Herrerasaurus lived about 230 million years ago.

One of the last kinds of dinosaur was the Tyrannosaurus.

Some dinosaurs were vegetarians.

They ate only plants.

Creatures that eat only plants are called 'herbivores'.

Some of the larger vegeterian dinosaurs had weak teeth.

Because of their weak teeth they swallowed their plants without chewing them.

Vegeterian dinosaurs also had wide mouths for gathering leaves. They had big cheeks to hold large mouthfuls of food.

Vegeterian dinosaurs had little claws on their toes. They used their claws to rip down tough leaves.

Some dinosaurs were meat-eaters, or 'carnivores'.

These dinosaurs travelled in packs and hunted smaller dinosaurs.

The carnivorous dinosaurs had sharp, jagged teeth to tear and bite.

They had sharp claws, with one large talon on each foot.

The talons were as long as five inches, and were used for slicing into the flesh of the animal to be eaten.

Extend your skills

Connectives (linking words and phrases) can be used both to link ideas within sentences and to link paragraphs. Using different types of connectives can help you to express your ideas clearly in your writing.

The table below lists three different kinds of connective:

Qualifying	Comparing	Persuading
Completely	Equally	Of course
Slightly	Similarly	Obviously
Mostly	In the same way	Naturally
To some extent	Alternatively	Indeed
More importantly	However	However

- **Qualifying** connectives are used to explain which ideas are more important than others.

  To be an ideal student you need to work very hard. **Slightly** more important than that, you need to let your teachers see that you are working hard. **Most** importantly, you must hand all of your work in on time.

- **Comparing** connectives are used when two or more things are being compared.

  I really enjoy spaghetti bolognaise. **Equally**, I enjoy other pasta dishes. **However**, my favourite meal has to be a rump steak and chips.

- **Persuading** connectives are used when the writer wants the readers to change their minds, or wants them to agree with the point that is being made.

  Everyone should take recycling seriously. **Indeed**, if we don't take it seriously we will be damaging our environment. **However**, there are signs that we youngsters are setting a good example.

1   Look at the three pieces of writing below. Each of them requires connectives to link the ideas together. See if you can select the right connectives to complete them.

> Although we all like to travel by car there are alternatives. For example, we could all be taking the opportunity to walk those short distances such as down to the local shop, or even to school each day. _____, we should be looking at the bicycle as an alternative form of transport; not only is the bicycle a greener option, it contributes to our general fitness. _____, if it is necessary to take a long journey, it is environmentally more friendly to take public transport than your own car.

> If you find yourself in a house fire do not panic. Or _____, try to make sure that nobody else panics. _____, check where the fire is strongest and move away from this area.

> Statistically, smoking is the biggest killer that you are ever likely to face. Did you know that 450 children start smoking in the United Kingdom, every day? _____, they don't care about their health: about half of all smokers will die because of this filthy habit. _____, 90% of lung cancer deaths and 80% of deaths from bronchitis are the result of smoking. _____, local doctors offer a wide range of support for those who want to give up.

Support

The first text compares different types of transport, so what type of connectives do you think you need?

The last extract tries to encourage people not to smoke. What type of connectives do you think you need?

2   Using the information from the first text, draft a short letter to parents from the head teacher persuading students to use environmentally-friendly forms of transport to get to school. Think about the connectives you should use to link the paragraphs in your letter.

Apply your learning

Task You have been asked to write an opinion column for a new newspaper for young people. The column is called 'Sounding Off' and the editor has asked you to write about reality TV shows, such as *The X Factor* and *I'm a Celebrity...Get me Out of Here!* The editor has given you a 250-word limit for the column.

First of all, decide what your point of view is. Do you think reality TV shows humiliate people or are they just good entertainment? Brainstorm your ideas on this topic and then start to think about how you could organise these in your writing. You could also use the internet to research the topic further.

Think about:

- how paragraphs work and make sure you know when to start a new one

- how you can link your ideas within paragraphs and make sure you avoid repetition

- how you can use connectives to make links between paragraphs.

Assess to Progress

How well can you use paragraphs to organise your writing now? Think about the writing that you have completed in this unit. Look back at the ratings you gave yourself at the beginning of the unit and decide whether any of them should change. Be ready to prove to a partner that your scores are realistic.

1	2	3	4	5	6	7

I find this difficult.　　　I'm getting there.　　　I'm good at this.

- I can organise different texts into paragraphs.

- I can link sentences within paragraphs.

- I can use connectives to link paragraphs.

You have volunteered to help your local youth group to attract more members. They have produced a leaflet, but it is not written in paragraphs and is therefore difficult to follow. You say that you will help to improve it.

Read the text and decide:

a) how many paragraphs it should be organised into

b) where each new paragraph should begin.

The Busbridge Youth Group needs you. We are a small group of enthusiastic 11-16 year olds. We meet every Monday night and play games, have discussions and take on projects for local people. Sounds boring? You'd be surprised how much fun it is. You're part of a group, no-one is made to feel like an outsider, and we get to do some great things. For example last year we all went out to see a West End Show, we did some high-wire team-building at "Go Ape" and we helped to fix up the garden at a local old people's home. We're always looking out for new members. To join, you just have to let us know. There's a 50 pence membership fee each week which we use to buy coffee and rent the hall, but everything else is paid for. Interested? Feel free to come along on your own or with a friend and we'll make you feel welcome and get you involved. You'll soon wonder why you hadn't joined years ago.

Writing AF5
Progress in ... *Varying sentence length and structure*

- Build different types and lengths of sentences.
- Pack more information and description into your sentences.
- Choose the best type of sentence to use for specific purposes.
- Use verbs accurately to refer to past, present or future.

Activate your learning

Rewrite the report below so that it has only four sentences. You can:

- add or take out words
- join sentences together and move them around
- change the punctuation.

Spaced-out spiders

NASA Scientists have found a new use for spiders.
They can use spiders to test for illegal drugs.
Spiders normally spin the same web pattern all the time.
When spiders are given a drug they no longer spin the same web pattern.
Scientists found that each drug causes a particular web pattern to be spun.
This is great.
Using spiders will be much cheaper than the traditional chemical tests.

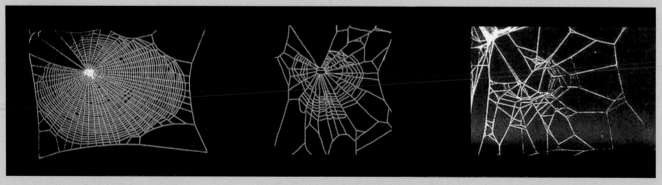

| Drug-free spider's web | The effect of marijuana | The effect of caffeine |

Assess to Progress

How confident are you about writing different types of sentence already? For each of the skills below, rate yourself by deciding which number on the scale shows your skill level best. Look back at what you wrote for the spider's web report on page 187 to find evidence to help you decide.

1	2	3	4	5	6	7

I find this difficult.   I'm getting there.   I'm good at this.

- I can write in complete sentences.

- I know how to use connectives to write longer sentences: **and, but, or, because, if, when, so**.

- I write verbs that are correct for the number of people doing the action, and for when, events are happening, e.g. **He jumps** over the fences easily. **They jump** over the fences easily.

- I can use different sentence lengths and structures to create specific effects.

Build your skills

Skilful writers know how to build different types and lengths of sentence. They choose the right kind of sentence to make their meaning clear and to create the right effect for their audience. Discover how to do this by following the skill steps to improve the draft advertisement at the top of the next page.

Step 1 Use simple sentences to grab attention

When you want to punch home a point or grab a reader's attention, use a short simple sentence. A simple sentence has one clause (a group of words that makes sense on its own).

1   Why do you think a simple sentence has been used for the heading?

2   Write two other simple sentences that could begin this advertisement, e.g. Do spiders ...?

3   Find two other simple sentences used in the advertisement.

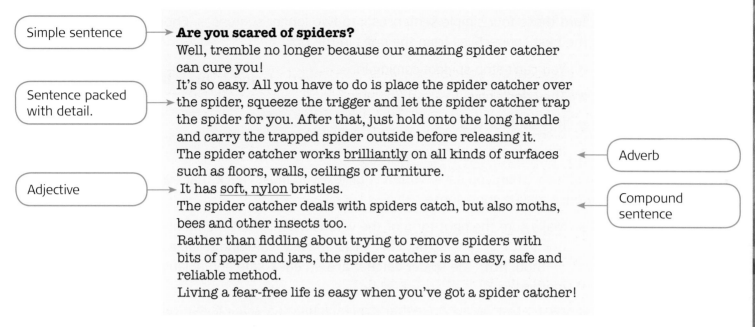

Simple sentence → **Are you scared of spiders?**

Well, tremble no longer because our amazing spider catcher can cure you!

Sentence packed with detail. → It's so easy. All you have to do is place the spider catcher over the spider, squeeze the trigger and let the spider catcher trap the spider for you. After that, just hold onto the long handle and carry the trapped spider outside before releasing it.

The spider catcher works <u>brilliantly</u> on all kinds of surfaces such as floors, walls, ceilings or furniture. ← Adverb

Adjective → It has <u>soft, nylon</u> bristles.

The spider catcher deals with spiders catch, but also moths, bees and other insects too. ← Compound sentence

Rather than fiddling about trying to remove spiders with bits of paper and jars, the spider catcher is an easy, safe and reliable method.

Living a fear-free life is easy when you've got a spider catcher!

Step 2   Make your sentences work hard

Avoid boring readers by rambling on and on. Instead, keep their attention by giving them information as quickly as possible. Do this by making your sentences work hard. Pack them with:

● more detail, e.g. 'such as floors, walls, ceilings ...'

● adjectives (words that describe a noun), e.g. 'soft nylon bristles'

● adverbs (words that describe a verb), e.g. 'works brilliantly'.

1   Write two more information-packed sentences that:

    a)   describe the length of the spider catcher e.g. 'It is...'

    b)   describe the speed of the spider catcher's trigger.
       e.g. 'The trigger works...'

Step 3   Use compound and complex sentences

Two main clauses can be linked together to form a compound sentence. You can use the connectives 'and', 'but' or 'or' to do this. Read the writer's explanation of the choices he made.

I could write two simple sentences:

The spider catcher deals with spiders. It can catch moths, bees and other insects too.

Connecting them with 'but' to build a compound sentence helps me show my reader just how useful the spider catcher could be.

The spider catcher deals with spiders, but also catches moths, bees and other insects too.

1 Turn these four simple sentences into two longer sentences. Choose the best connectives from the ones in the box:

- You can't stop spiders coming in.
- They don't have to stay.
- It is safe for you.
- It is safe for spiders.

and	or	but

Remember, when you have written your text you must check that every sentence makes good sense:

- Make sure the right form of the verb is used to suit the number doing it, e.g. 'The spider catcher **is** an easy, safe and reliable method' **not** 'The spider catcher **are** an easy, safe and reliable method'.

- Look carefully for clues that tell you when the event is happening, e.g. today, yesterday, tomorrow, last night, in the future, later on. Then check that the verb is in the right tense.

- When you want to build longer sentences, for example, to add an explanation, to persuade or to argue, these connectives are really useful because they tell your readers how your ideas link together:

because	although	if	when	since	so	while	after
unless	on the one hand		on the other hand		for this reason		

2 Look at the list of connectives above. Which ones do you know and use in your writing already? Which ones are you less sure about using?

3 You are going to write four sentences arguing that a spider catcher is a must-have item for everyone's home.

a) Write two sentences using connectives you are already comfortable with.

b) Write two sentences using connectives that you are less sure about.

Support

In an **argument** which connectives could you use to show readers:
a) these two points are opposite?
b) the next part of the sentence is why I have this opinion?

Reinforce your skills

Work in groups as you practise building different types and lengths of sentence to suit different purposes and audiences.

Timbertops advertises dogs who are trained to be used by film or TV producers. They have drafted descriptions for two of their dogs but it isn't easy for readers to tell the difference between them.

1   Rewrite the two descriptions to make the dogs and their abilities seem very different. Add details to the highlighted nouns.

Jack and I had a time when we were working on the set of *Calendar Girls*. Jack was a greyhound – he had intelligence and a willingness to please everyone who had a kind word for him.

Popsie, a Jack Russell cross poodle, was the star of *Hollyoaks*. Popsie has appeared in productions, adverts and promotions. He is trained and so eager to please.

2   The author of the text below is a film dog trainer. Here she explains how she trained Tara to perform some of the typical tricks used in film work. Where should she use the connectives in the box below in her sentences?

| because | although | if | when | since | so | while | after | unless |

_____ you see your pet on TV or in a film it is a great feeling. It has been easy to train Tara for film work _____ she loves food and enjoys doing tricks for me. _____ teaching her to do simple tricks, such as jumping over obstacles, she found jumping in and out of moving cars, leaping over people and other dogs easy.

_____ we were preparing for her last film, I taught her to jump through hoops wrapped with cling film _____ she would find jumping through a window easy. She also practised working with A frames _____ this is a good way to prepare a dog to walk along narrow walls etc. _____ I haven't trained Tara to do bite work yet I am sure she will have no problems learning it _____ her next movie role requires it. A dog won't perform well _____ it is happy and relaxed.

Stretch

How could changing the sentence types and connectives help the writer to turn this into a **persuasive** text to encourage people to train their pets? Rewrite the first paragraph, beginning 'If you want to see your pet ...'

3 Play Sentence Bingo. Write six long sentences that discuss this question:

Is it right to train animals to perform in circuses, films, and so on, just to entertain people?

Each sentence must use a different connective from the bingo card below. The winner is the first one to use up six connectives and call out 'Bingo'.

because	although	if	while
when	since	so	unless

Extend your skills

In the extract opposite from the novel *The Secret Heart*, the writer David Almond is describing someone being hunted by a tiger. Complete the following activities to find out how he uses different types of sentence to make his description really effective. Then borrow his techniques as you prepare to write your own story.

1 Work in groups.

a) Search the text carefully to find as many examples as you can of sentences packed with:

- powerful verbs to describe the action
- lists of striking adjectives that describe the tiger's features
- details telling readers more about the tiger's actions.

b) Discuss which tasks each of these types of sentence are used for:

Types of sentence

- Short simple sentences
- Sentences packed with information
- Longer sentences using connectives to link points

Tasks

- Helping readers picture the tiger better
- Describing the tiger's movements
- Making the action seem really tense

The tiger padded through the night. Joe Maloney smelt it, the hot, sour breath, the stench of its pelt. The odour crept through the streets, through his open window and into his dreams. He felt the animal wildness on his tongue, in his nostrils. The tiger moved as if it knew him, as if it was drawn to him. Joe heard its footpads on the stairs. He heard its long slow breath, the distant sighing in its lungs, the rattle in its throat. It came inside. It filled the bedroom. The huge head hung over him. The glittering cruel eyes stared into him. The hot tongue, harsh as sandpaper, licked his arm. The mouth was wide open, the curved teeth were poised to close on him. He prepared to die.

2   You are going to write a half-page description of a nightmare in which you are being chased by a fierce animal.

a) Spend a few minutes deciding where the chase is happening, what animal is chasing you and why it is so terrifying.

b) Jot down lots of vivid verbs you can use to describe the animal's movement as it comes towards you, e.g. raced, stalked, pounced, snarled, loomed above.

c) Use a frame like the one below to help you build some vivid descriptive phrases which you can pack into your longer sentences.

Animal's features	Description	Animal's actions	Description
eyes	Glittering, cruel ...	glaring	fiercely, pinning me to the spot
teeth	Sharp as blades		
claws...			
connectives	where	when	which as if

d) Now start to write your description. Your nightmare begins as you realise the animal is coming towards you. Write a short simple sentence that you can use to begin your description,

e.g. A claw tore ...

e) Choose three powerful verbs you jotted down in your table and use them to write longer detailed sentences describing the fearsome animal as it chases you,

e.g. Clawing at ...

f) Use some of the verbs you chose earlier to write a group of three short sentences that will build a feeling of tension as the animal gets closer and closer to you during your description.

g) Your nightmare ends as the animal catches you. Write the short simple sentence that will end your nightmare.

3 Check through your draft to make sure:

● you have used different sorts of sentence for maximum effect

● each sentence makes good sense

● your verbs are written in the right way to show readers who is doing the action and when and where the action takes place.

Apply your learning

Task Now you are going to plan, draft and write an advertisement that will sell this Bug Zapper to people from a wide range of age groups, from kids to grannies. Make sure your final draft uses different types and lengths of sentence and the right forms of verbs.

1 a) As you plan your advertisement, use these questions to help you decide what information you should include to attract readers:

● What does the Bug Zapper do?

● What type of people might enjoy using it?

● How might they use it?

● How will the Bug Zapper change their lives?

b) You could also brainstorm lists of powerful words you can use to describe the Bug Zapper, using the Bug Zapper and the insects that readers want to get rid of.

2 As you draft your advertisement, think carefully about:

- which types of sentence you will use
- which connectives will help readers to understand how your ideas are linked
- what details and description you want to include.

3 When you have completed your draft, reread your advertisement to check that every sentence makes good sense and that verbs are correct. Remember to vary the types of sentences you use in your advertisement.

Assess to Progress

How good are you now at:

- adding detail and description to sentences
- using a variety of connectives, e.g. if, when, because
- changing the tense of your verbs in a way that makes sure your meaning is still clear?

1 Look back at the original ratings you gave yourself on page 188.

a) Rate yourself again for each of the skills listed above.

b) Discuss your ratings with a partner. Demonstrate why/how your rating has improved using examples from your advertisement.

e.g. This sentence shows that ...

2 Work with a partner. Use the checklist below to help you discuss ways in which you could improve some of the sentences in your Bug Zapper adverts.

- Did you use simple sentences to grab readers' attention or end the advert with a ringing last sentence?
- Are there any sentences you could pack with more detail?
- What connectives have you used to build longer sentences? Have you used some new connectives that you weren't using before you began this unit?
- Were all your verbs in the right tense?

3 Use what you have discovered to help each other set a target that will help you keep on trying to use different types of sentence in your writing.

e.g. By next week's lesson I will have practised ... and be able to show you ...

You have been asked to redesign the School Council page of your school website. The problem is that the current version has very little sentence variety. This makes it pretty boring to read. Your job is to edit the content to make it more interesting.

1 Read the current web page and see how you can improve it. Aim to:

  ▸ create some short, simple sentences

  ▸ create some complex sentences so that there are subordinate clauses

  ▸ add or delete any description inside the sentences that you think doesn't work well

  ▸ make sure you use the correct verb tenses in your sentences.

2 Add a section to the web page giving pupils instructions about how they can apply to become members of the School Council. Think about the types of sentence you should use to make the instructions clear.

Goosegog High

"Specialists in Maths and English"

Head teacher. Miss S. Payne BSc (HONS)

Goosegog High

Tel: 01182 999 1112   Fax: 01182 999 1123   admin@goosego.mars.sch.uk

---

Home › Schools Council

MAIN MENU	Schools Council
■ Home	
■ Contact	Welcome to the School Council web page and we hope you will enjoy reading about all the things that we have been doing since last September. School Council is made up of representatives from each year in the school and we meet once a week during tutor time and discuss issues that are important. Recently these issues have included improving the school environment, for example by making sure the toilets always have soap and toilet paper, starting a paper recycling scheme, doing a consultation about what pupils think of the current school uniform, and looking at ways of making the school catering more attractive and better value. We have also run various charity events including non-uniform days, cake stalls and a Christmas Show which was really popular and raised over £300 for local charities. School Council is chaired by Head Girl and Head Boy, Charlie and Jason, and they meet the head teacher once a month to pass on our views and give advice on how we think the school could be improved.
■ Documents	
■ Gallery	
■ Schools Council	
■ Holidays	
■ Job Vacancies	
■ LRC	
■ Links	
■ Location	
■ Mission Statement	
■ News Archive	
■ Search Engines	
■ Subscribe	
■ 6th form	
	Keep checking back on this page and you will see all the other projects we are involved in and find out more about the progress we are making.

Writing AF6

Progress in ... Using punctuation accurately

Activate your learning

How well do you know when to use different punctuation marks? Well enough to win a million pounds? Play the game below and find out. Work in teams to see how many of the sentences you can complete correctly.

An exclamation mark is used to show ___
_____
£100

A question mark is used to show ____
_____
£200

One use of a full stop is to show _____
_____
£300

A second use of a full stop is to show ____
_____
£500

A third use of a full stop is to show _____
_____
£1000

A sentence should always begin with __
and end with_____
£2000

Commas are used to separate items in a_____
£4000

The personal pronoun 'I' should always be written as a_____

£8000

Inverted commas ' ' are placed at the ___ and _____ of_____, and around _____

£16,000

The first word written in speech should always begin with a_____

£25,000

When writing speech in the middle of a sentence, a__is needed before opening__

£500,000

Commas are used to separate sections of a sentence so that _____

£100,000

A comma is usually needed before writing the connective introducing a _____ clause.

£1,000,000

Assess to Progress

How good are you at these skills already? Do you use the correct punctuation and check your writing for accuracy?

Decide how highly you should rate yourself on the scale below.

| 1 | 2 | 3 | 4 | 5 | 6 | 7 |

I find this difficult.　　　I'm getting there.　　　I'm good at this.

- I know what kinds of meaning different punctuation marks are meant to show, e.g. beginning a word with a capital letter to show a word is someone's name.

- I know how to use commas to separate out items in lists and different chunks of meaning in a sentence.

- I know when to use each of the punctuation marks that can end a sentence, e.g. ? to mark the end of a question.

- I always punctuate speech correctly.

- I always proofread my work and correct it to make sure my spelling, grammar and punctuation is correct and every sentence makes sense.

Build your skills

1 When you write something, you want your reader to understand you easily. Punctuating your sentences correctly helps to make the meaning clear. Read the extract below and complete the comments.

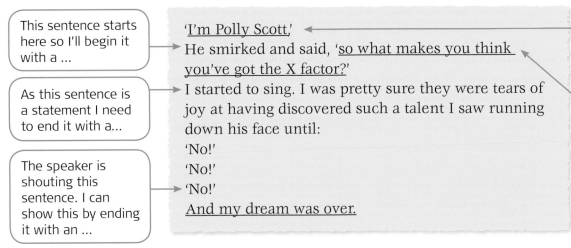

> This sentence starts here so I'll begin it with a ...

> As this sentence is a statement I need to end it with a...

> The speaker is shouting this sentence. I can show this by ending it with an ...

'I'm Polly Scott,'
He smirked and said, 'so what makes you think you've got the X factor?'
I started to sing. I was pretty sure they were tears of joy at having discovered such a talent I saw running down his face until:
'No!'
'No!'
'No!'
And my dream was over.

> The name of the person in this sentence needs to begin with ...

> These words are being spoken by someone, so I need to ...

The best way to make sure your writing is as accurate as possible is to proofread your work, over and over. Use the following steps every time you check your work.

Step 1 Does it makes sense?

Will what I have written make sense to the reader? Make sure you read what is actually on the page, not what you think you have written.

Step 2 Punctuation check

Have I put in all the punctuation that is needed to make my meaning clear?

Step 3 Spelling check

Do any of the words look like they might be spelt wrong?

Step 4 Grammar check

- Does it sound right?
- Do I think the grammar is right?
- Does each sentence have a verb?
- Is it clear who or what is carrying out the verb?
- Is the verb expressed in the right way for that number of people?

Reinforce your skills

Sometimes there are very clear punctuation rules for you to follow. For example, you should always:

- use commas to separate the items on a list, e.g. In the box I packed a round of cheese sandwiches, cakes, an apple, crisps and a bottle of water.

- use a comma before opening speech marks when the speech is part of a sentence, e.g. 'Your books are pretty good,' she wrote, 'except for the total lack of motorbikes.'

- use a comma to separate information in a sentence so that the meaning is clearer, e.g.

> The packed lunch, which I was meant to take on the school trip, lay forgotten on the breakfast bar.

The pair of commas is used to separate out the information about what was meant to happen to the packed lunch from the information about where the packed lunch had been left.

> The packed lunch which I was meant to take on the school trip, lay forgotten on the breakfast bar.

By using no commas, the writer is showing that there was more than one packed lunch to choose from, so he picked up the one that was meant to be taken on the school trip.

Choosing the right punctuation to use is not always as easy as just following a rule. Sometimes it is a case of deciding what punctuation you need to use to show readers what your sentence really means.

Support

Where are the commas needed in the following sentence:
At the bus stop which is a ten minute walk from our house I realised I had forgotten my lunch box.
What are the two different ideas in the sentence?

1   Look at each of the pairs of sentences that follow. For each one, discuss the following questions:

● How does the change in punctuation give each sentence a different meaning?

● What is the rule for deciding how to use punctuation in each case?

The first example has been completed to help you.

a)   **'She's your girlfriend.' 'She's your girlfriend?'**

In the first sentence the speaker is just stating a fact. In the second sentence he's asking a question as if he can't believe it.

Rule: Putting a question mark at the end of a statement lets your reader know that the speaker is asking whether it is true.

b)   Josh kissed Ellie, and her friend Ben began to laugh.
     Josh kissed Ellie and her friend, Ben began to laugh.

c)   The teacher said the student is wacky.
     The teacher, said the student, is wacky.

d)   The students who ate all my chocolates deserve a detention.
     The students, who ate all my chocolates, deserve a detention.

Support

How many students will get detention in each sentence? All of them or only the chocolate eaters? What does the pair of commas show readers in the second sentence?

Extend your skills

1 Read the text below, which is taken from author Morris Gleitzman's *bits of an autobiography I may not write*. Answer the questions in boxes around the text to explore how he used punctuation to make his meaning clear.

> How else could Morris Gleitzman have punctuated the first paragraph? What is emphasised to readers by the way it is punctuated?

Two weeks of thinking, and still no idea for my next book. I'd tried everything. Meditation. Self hypnosis. Vacuuming my scalp to stimulate my brain.

Then a letter arrived from a kid in Western Australia. 'Your books are pretty good,' she wrote, 'except for the total lack of motorbikes.'

> Why are inverted commas used here?

> Why is this comma needed here?

I fell to my knees, partly in gratitude and partly because the vacuum cleaner was still on my head. At last a story idea. A kid travelling across the Great Sandy Desert on a motorbike.

2 The next part of the text is about how another letter that Morris Gleitzman receives influences his writing. Here is a copy of the letter:

> Dear Morris Gleitzman,
>
> I live in Adelaide. I think your books are reasonably okay but why so few exotic fish?
>
> Yours truly
>
> A fan

Working in pairs, write the next part of the text, with Gleitzman explaining how he is going to work the exotic fish into his story. Think about how you should use punctuation to make what is happening in the story clear to the reader. You should start like this:

I'd just finished Chapter One when the next letter came...

Support

Morris Gleitzman writes his fans' suggestions as if they are spoken aloud, so remember to punctuate any quotes as speech.

3 The cartoon below shows you how Morris Gleitzman reacts to his fans' comments.

Work in pairs to write the text of this part of the story. Make sure you use punctuation correctly to help your readers understand your meaning. The paragraph should include:

- Gleitzman receiving a fan letter from Bristol with the elderly woman's words (in the cartoon caption) written as speech.

- Gleitzman's idea of how he can include her suggestion in the story he is writing.

4 Below is a draft version of the end of the text. Use the steps on page 199 to help you to rewrite the draft so that it is clearly expressed and correctly punctuated.

It looked like she were a goner until the letter from philadelphia arrived. More sports it said. Which is how, in the next draft the kids came to have a table-tennis bat handy to whack Gran on the back.

Shouldn't you be thinking up your own ideas, Dad asked the kids. Why I replied.

Oh, No reason,' they shrugged, handing me six letters.

Water –ski-ing said one. clydesdale horses said another Self reticulating irrigation systems said the other four.

This morning when the postman came I hid under my desk he found me I were sobbing.

Must be tuff being a writer he said bending down and handing me a bundle of letters I wouldn't know where to get the ideas from

Apply your learning

Task 1 Working on your own, write a conversation between two famous people. You could present it as a playscript or the opening of a novel. Give it the title, *Scandal*. The conversation can be about anyone and anything you like, for example:

- Footballers discussing match fixing

- Famous film stars swapping gossip

- A journalist interviewing a politician who reveals an important secret about the Prime Minister

- Top models plotting to stop a new girl from becoming more famous than them.

  Try to use a range of punctuation. You should use punctuation to help the reader hear how the characters are speaking, e.g. a comma could show a pause in speech or an exclamation mark show somebody shouting.

2 After you have finished writing, give your work a final, careful proofread to check that the grammar, spelling and punctuation are accurate and make your meaning clear. Make any necessary changes in pencil and underline them. These changes will prove to you how good your proofreading skills are.

Assess to Progress

Look carefully at the conversation you have just written. Look at each of the statements below and decide where you would rate yourself now on the scale. How good are you now at:

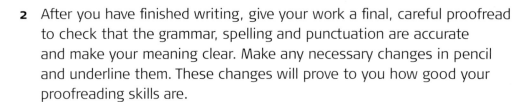

| 1 | 2 | 3 | 4 | 5 | 6 | 7 |

I find this difficult.   I'm getting there.   I'm good at this.

- using the correct punctuation marks to show readers the beginning and end of your sentences and making your meaning clear

- using commas to separate items in lists, make your meaning clear, and to change the emphasis in a sentence

- writing speech using accurate punctuation

- proofreading your work so that the grammar, spelling and punctuation are accurate and your meaning is clear?

SKILLS FOR LIFE

You are the captain of the school football team. The school webteam has asked you to provide a match report for the weekly web bulletin. One of the team has volunteered to write the report, but has accidentally saved it in a text-only format. The content is good, but difficult to follow without the punctuation.

1 Read the report through and add in the necessary punctuation so it can be published.

Ten-man Walton High staged a superb fight back yesterday achieving a great win even though earlier they had looked dead and buried against high-flying Troston College goals from Tom Skevington in the first half then Elliott Henwood shortly after the restart set Troston on the way to victory then suddenly Tony Joyce gave Walton High hope when he pulled one back Simon Rees hit a deserved equaliser and Joyce popped up again with a late winner to seal an amazing triumph interviewed after the match Tony Joyce said we were really helped by the home crowd they got behind us from the start and never lost confidence PE teacher mr Walden said we are all delighted with this result which gets us a step nearer the county finals final score Walton High 2 Troston College 3

2 Now write the opening paragraph for a report of a sporting event that you have watched. Try to use a range of punctuation.

Writing AF7

Progress in ... Using vocabulary precisely

LEARNING OBJECTIVES

- Use words precisely to make your meaning clear and create specific effects.
- Draw on your own knowledge and reading to use the right words at the right time.
- Use a thesaurus and other sources to extend your vocabulary.

Activate your learning

Work with a partner for this vocabulary quiz, taking it in turns to answer the questions. You have to choose the correct meaning for each of the words. See how many points each of you can get.

Here's an example to show you how:

Blouse (a) a breed of dog (b) a girl's shirt (c) a flower

Answer: (b) a girl's shirt

1 **allow** (a) everyone (b) give permission (c) try hard

2 **improbable** (a) not likely (b) impossible (c) can't be moved

3 **fatality** (a) very attractive (b) a death (c) a good idea

4 **temporary** (a) not permanent (b) in fashion (c) dangerous

5 **simultaneous** (a) lives in the sea (b) at the same time (c) one after another

6 **locate** (a) find (b) fix (c) try

7 **bleak** (a) feeble (b) whine (c) cold and unpleasant

8 **commence** (a) give a comment (b) to start (c) avoid

9 **portly** (a) fairly fat (b) heavily (c) greatly

10 **reprimand** (a) put first (b) give an order (c) tell someone off

Assess to Progress

How good are you already at choosing the right words in your own writing? Can you choose the best words to express your ideas clearly or to create special effects? Think about the vocabulary quiz you have just played and any writing that you have done recently. Then rate yourself for the following skills using the scale below:

| 1 | 2 | 3 | 4 | 5 | 6 | 7 |

I find this difficult.   I'm getting there.   I'm good at this.

- I can usually find the best word to use when I write.

  Self-check: For example, I used ...

- When I come across a new word, when I am reading, I usually look it up.

  Self-check: For example, when I came across the word ...

- I know how to use different sources to help me find the right word.

  Self-check: For example, if I was to start to use certain words too often I know how to use a thesaurus to help me find alternatives.

Build your skills

Choosing the right words can make your writing much more effective. Raj has written to the school governors arguing against their policy on wearing school uniforms.

1 Read the extract from Raj's letter on the next page, then answer the questions in the boxes.

2 Find three examples of formal style in the letter. Hint: this could be the way sentences are constructed, as well as words or phrases used. For each example, explain why you think that this is a good style of language for Raj's letter to his head teacher.

'Claim' suggests that schools are wrong. What would the word 'argue' suggest?

The word 'students' makes the pupils sound older and more mature. What word would have made them sound younger?

This connective links the paragraphs together. What other connectives can you think of that link ideas together?

'Make' suggests that the students are being made to do this unfairly. Can you think of a similar word?

'Hope' suggests that this will never happen. Can you think of a different word that would fit here?

This suggests that it is a ridiculous argument without actually saying that it is. How could this point be made in a different way?

Schools <u>claim</u> that school uniform is a very good thing for <u>students</u>. However, I think that there are more reasons why we shouldn't have school uniform than there are in favour of it.

One reason that schools <u>make</u> students wear school uniform is so that the students all look the <u>same</u>. Teachers <u>hope</u> that if we all look the same we will behave the same and consequently work hard. However, I feel that if schools want us to think independently we should be allowed to dress independently.

<u>Another reason</u> that schools like school uniform is because they say that students will feel proud of their school. This <u>cannot be a serious argument</u>, as if students are not proud of their uniform how could they ever be proud of their school?

3 Now look at this extract from a letter that Kara wrote about school uniform. Look at the underlined words and phrases. Explain why they are not good choices, and see if you can suggest better words and phrases.

Schools say that school uniform is a very good thing for <u>pupils</u>. But I think that is <u>rubbish</u>. There's loads more reasons against school uniform than there are in favour of it.

One reason that schools make children wear school uniform is so that the children all look the same. Teachers hope that if we all look the same we will behave the same and consequently work hard. <u>But I reckon</u>, if we all look the same then <u>we'll</u> all think the same and no-one will come up with an original idea.

<u>One reason</u> that schools like school uniform is so that pupils will feel proud of their school. And this is <u>a load of tripe</u> as well. <u>Kids</u> hate the uniform and even hate coming to school.

Reinforce your skills

A wide vocabulary helps you to choose the most appropriate words for different situations. There are many different words that have similar meanings. These are called **synonyms**. There are different sources you can use that will help you find synonyms to add variety to your writing.

Using a computer: If you are working in a word-processing package, such as Word, you can right-click on a word and select 'Synonyms'. By doing this you will be provided with a list of words with the same meanings. Look at this example.

A pupil wanted to find a synonym for 'run'.
Using a thesaurus: A thesaurus presents words in alphabetical order, like a dictionary, but it provides synonyms instead of definitions. For example, if you looked up 'run' in a thesaurus you might see something like this:

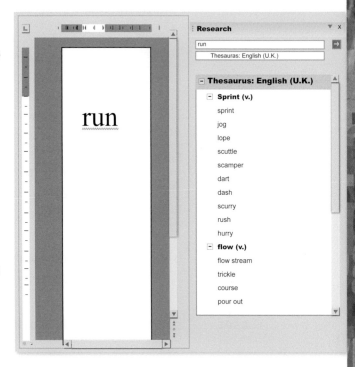

run (v) dash, scurry, sprint, jog

The (v) tells you that the word 'run' is a verb or action word. The words **dash**, **scurry**, **sprint** and **jog** are all synonyms for **run**.

1 Work with a partner for this activity. Imagine that you are writing the text for an advertisement for a new fizzy drink aimed at teenagers. Some members of the public have tested samples of the drink, and this is how they have described it:

> It is a brown drink that is very sugary but there is an acidic aftertaste.

> It is bubbly and makes a fizzing noise when the can is opened.

> When it is cold it tastes refreshing.

a) You need to persuade teenagers to buy the drink by choosing the most appealing words to describe it. To help you think about all the different words you could use to describe the drink, create a table like the one below.

Target word	Synonyms	Your choice of synonym
Brown		
Sugary		
Acidic		
Fizzy		
Taste		
Refreshing		

b) Fill in the second column of the table with one synonym for each of the target words selected from the list below.

russet　　sparkling　　stimulating　　sharp　　sweet　　effervescent　　flavour

Support

Use a dictionary to check the definition for any word you don't know the meaning of.

c) For each of the target words, find at least three more synonyms and add these to the second column of the table. You could use a thesaurus to help you.

d) Which of the synonyms would have the most appeal for a teenage audience? Discuss your ideas and for each target word fill in the final column with the best synonym.

2 Rewrite the description of the drink. As well as changing the target words, think about any other vocabulary changes you could make to make the description more appealing to teenagers.

Stretch

The advertising company has decided to market the drink as an energy drink for sports people. Look back at your description.
- Which details would you want to change?
- Which words could you use to appeal to this new audience?

Extend your skills

As well as using resources such as a thesaurus, there are other techniques you can use to improve your vocabulary. Asking other people to read and comment on the vocabulary you have chosen can help you to think about the effect of the words on a reader. When you complete a first draft, ask a friend to read it and suggest any words you can change to improve the effectiveness of your writing.

1   In pairs, read the extract below from a piece of creative writing that Sue handed in to her teacher. Sue's task was to describe a scene that she knew well. The teacher has added some comments to Sue's writing. Help Sue to improve her piece of writing by answering the questions from her teacher.

> Can you think of a more powerful word than 'scary'?

> Can you think of an adjective to describe the dark, like 'frightening dark'?

> I like the idea of the trees grabbing you. However, can you think of a more powerful verb than 'grab'?

The wood is a scary place. Tall trees bow down to make a covering that blocks out the sky. In the dark you can see shadows that seem to dance in front of you like whispers. They try to grab you as you walk amongst them. On the ground, beneath your feet, the earth seems alive as mice, voles and even snakes move around in the grass. But even so, whenever I visit this wood I feel good because it seems that I am the only person there.

Sue, this is a good piece of writing. However, I think that you need to develop your vocabulary to make it even more effective. Look at the words that I have underlined and see if you can find some more interesting or powerful words.

> 'bow down' doesn't sound very scary. What other phrase can you use to suggest that the trees are scary?

> Can you think of more powerful words than 'move' and 'good'? These words don't really tell the reader very much.

Support

See if you can help Sue by choosing more interesting or powerful words to replace the words that her teacher has underlined. There are some suggestions below.

grasp   seize   terrify   threatening   crawl   creep   content
comfortable   gloom   murkiness   crouch   stoop

Text A

As soon as it was light they could see the forest coming as it were to meet them, or waiting for them like a black and frowning wall before them. The land began to slope up and up, and it seemed to the hobbit that a silence began to draw in upon them. Birds began to sing less. There were no more deer; not even rabbits to be seen. By the afternoon they had reached the eaves of Mirkwood, and were resting almost beneath the great overhanging boughs of its outer trees. Their trunks were huge and gnarled, their branches twisted, their leaves were dark and long. Ivy grew on them and trailed along the ground.

Text B

This is the forest primeval.
The murmuring pines and the hemlocks,
Bearded with moss, and in garments green,
indistinct in the twilight,
stand like harpers hoar,
with beards that rest on their bosoms.

You can also use the texts you read to help improve and expand your vocabulary, making a note of any memorable words and phrases you encounter and thinking about how you can use these in your own writing.

1   Look at the extracts opposite, both of which describe a forest. Text A is from *The Hobbit* by J.R.R. Tolkien and Text B is from *Evangeline* by Henry Wadsworth Longfellow.

2   Pick out any words that you are not sure of the meaning of. Discuss with a partner what you think each word could mean, then check the definition in a dictionary.

3   a) Pick out any words and phrases from the extracts that you think are particularly effective in creating an image of the forest in your mind. Compare your choices with a partner and discuss the reasons you selected these words.

    b) For one of the words or phrases you selected, write a sentence explaining how it helped you to picture the forest and what effect it created.

4   Using some of the words you have picked out, write your own brief description of a tree or forest. Use vocabulary that helps to create a scary atmosphere.

Apply your learning

Task   Write a description of a place you know well. You should:

-   include details that appeal to the reader's senses (sight, hearing, smell, taste, touch)

-   show how you feel about the place through the language you use. Think about what kind of atmosphere you want to create with the vocabulary you choose.

Consider how your choice of words can bring the place alive in the mind of the reader. You could present your description in the form of a poem, like the example opposite. You should use a thesaurus or other appropriate resources to help you make the best vocabulary choices.

Assess to Progress

How good are you now at:

- using words precisely to make your meaning clear and create specific effects

- using the right words at the right time

- using a thesaurus and other resources to extend your vocabulary?

Think about the description you have just written.

1 How easy did you find it to choose words deliberately for their impact? Complete the following sentences.

- The most important thing I have learnt about this is …

- What I need to do to improve this aspect of my writing is …

2 Have you shown evidence that your vocabulary has developed in your description? Complete these sentences:

- I have used the following words in my description that I haven't used before …

- What I need to do to improve this aspect of my writing is …

You have seen this advert for a part-time job at a local supermarket:

Sales assistant wanted

Busy supermarket seeks a hard-working and motivated person to work evening and weekend shifts. Good communication and customer care skills essential. You will be responsible for the pricing of goods, maintaining stock levels and providing customers with an excellent service. No previous experience necessary as full training will be given to the successful applicant.

If you are interested in the position, please write a short letter of application. Interviews will be conducted in two weeks' time.

Write a letter applying for this job. In it you should explain why you are interested in the job and why you should be invited for an interview. Think about who will be reading your letter and try to make them understand why you are the best person for the job. Try to choose the right tone for your letter and think about the words and phrases you can use to persuade them that you are the person they are looking for.

Writing AF8
Progress in ... Reviewing spelling

- Identify common spelling mistakes.
- Increase your knowledge of spelling patterns.
- Access a range of spelling skills to help you to remember difficult or unusual spellings.
- Improve the accuracy of your spelling by proofreading and making revisions.

Activate your learning

Look at the following piece of writing, which was word-processed. Although the spell-check hasn't picked up any errors at all, it is clear there are some spelling mistakes.

'Welcome to my home...'

The entrance too my house is threw my front garden. At this time of year, the garden is full of flour's and beautiful butterflies, busy bee's and nesting bird's. My front door is hidden away between ivy leave's witch climb up too my bedroom window. The door creak's open to reveal are hallway, which is quiet, peaceful and dark. You make your way threw all the coat's, Wellington's, scarves and hat's, before you come two the lounge. Their are to large settee's in here, wear we like to sit in the evening and watch television. They're is also a stereo and loads off cds in hear, as my dad loves listening two music. In are kitchen, their are lots of pot's, pan's and all off my mums plant's.

1 In pairs, spot all the spelling errors you can and list them next to the correct spelling.

2 Compare your error list with that of another pair. Discuss these questions:

- Why do you think the spell-check didn't pick up all of these errors?

- What does this mean you should do when writing using a computer?

Assess to Progress

How good are you at spelling already? Think about the writing that you do at school and at home, as well as the activity you have just completed. Then rate yourself from 1 to 7 for each of the following skills:

1	2	3	4	5	6	7

I find this difficult.　　　　I'm getting there.　　　　I'm good at this.

- I can spot when words are spelt incorrectly.
  e.g. I can spot when an apostrophe is in the wrong place.

- I can spell most common words correctly.
  e.g. I can spell words like 'target' and 'answering'.

- I can spell more complicated words correctly.
  e.g. I can spell words like 'exaggerate' and 'necessary'.

- When I proofread and revise my writing, I check for spelling errors.

- I use a range of ways of learning how to spell words correctly.
  e.g. recording in a book, spelling rules, silly rhymes.

Build your skills

Some spelling mistakes are a result of words that sound the same, but are spelt differently, being used incorrectly. These are called **homophones**. For example, the words 'there' and 'their' are very often mixed up. Here is one rule to help you use the right word in the right place:

> The word 'their' is always followed by a noun (a thing), because 'their' means 'something belonging to them', e.g. Their car was parked outside.
> The word 'there' is always followed by a word like 'is', 'are', 'was' or 'were', e.g. There is a car outside.

1　Use this rule to help you to spot which of the underlined words in the following sentences are spelt correctly, and which are misspelt:

- <u>There</u> are several places you can go in my house to get a bit of peace and quiet.

- <u>There</u> bedroom is the largest of the bedrooms.

- We have a garage next to the house, where my parents keep <u>their</u> car.

- <u>Their</u> is a large pond in my back garden.

2 Another pair of words that are very often confused is 'our' and 'are'. What rule could you create to help someone to use and spell these correctly? To help you, look at the following examples, which show the words being used correctly:

- Our house is covered in ivy leaves.

- There are several steps up to my front door.

- We are a very close family.

- When I first moved into our house, I hated it because it was horrible and dull.

Support

Look at the words that come after 'our'. Think about what type of word these are. Now look at the type of word that comes before 'are'. How might this help you to create a rule about when to use each word correctly?

Stretch

Can you think of any other words that you confuse and use incorrectly? Try and develop a rule to help you to use the right word in the right place. Look through something you are currently reading and pick out examples that support your rule.

Now look at the following piece of writing and the spelling errors that have been identified.

> When this person has written 'field' they have mixed up the 'ie' spelling.

Our garden has a long driveway through it, and the lawn is as big as a <u>feild</u>. My mum likes to keep it looking nice and she grows lots of plants and flowers to keep it looking good. All our <u>naybours</u> are <u>jelous</u> because <u>are</u> garden is nicer than <u>theres</u>.

When you get to <u>are door</u>, <u>their</u> is a big door <u>nocker</u> in the shape of a lion's head.

> 'Jealous' isn't a common word, but it has a missing vowel here.

> This person gets mixed up with 'are' and 'our' and 'there' and 'their'.

> Although the ending of 'neighbours' is right, the beginning is another 'ie' mistake. Maybe this person finds 'ie' spellings difficult.

> He or she has also missed off a silent letter in 'knocker'.

As well as confusing the words 'are' and 'our' and 'there' and 'their', this writer has also misspelt some words by getting the vowel combinations wrong. Look at the following examples of this type of error:

Error type	Misspelling	Correct spelling
Vowel combinations	naybours	neighbours
	cleen	clean
	neices	nieces

3   Now look at the next section of his or her writing. Pick out the spelling errors and create a table like the one above. Make sure that you identify the type of error and include the correct spelling. You should be able to find six errors in total.

> Inside the door, their are lots of brite colours. We where going to move house, but we decided to stay were we where, and my dad built an extension and a conservatry.

Stretch

Are any types of error repeated? If so, which ones? If you had to advise the writer about how to improve their spelling, what would you say?

Reinforce your skills

Making sure that different forms of a verb (action words) are spelt correctly can be difficult. Depending on how the verb is spelt, the rule can be different. Look at the following rules to help you to make sure you know how to spell the different parts of a verb correctly.

- Often you just add '-ing' and '-ed' to a verb, depending on the job it is doing in the sentence. For some words this is easy:
  e.g. form → forming, formed.

- When verbs end in a consonant, then a single vowel then a single consonant, you should double the consonant before you add '-ing' or '-ed': e.g. stab → stabbing, stabbed; fit → fitting, fitted.

- Many verbs end in -e. Here you drop the 'e' before you add '-ing', or '-ed':
  e.g. bake → baking, baked; pollute → polluting, polluted.

- Remember that many common words have different forms altogether when you use them to refer to the past:
  e.g. fight → fought; sink → sank.

1   Write a short description of your own home. Imagine you are writing a guide for someone who hasn't been there before. Include lots of adjectives and detail.

2   a) Proofread your piece of writing to identify any spelling errors. Slowly read what you have written out loud:

- Tick each word you know is spelt correctly
- Put a question mark over words that you are not sure about
- Put a cross over words you know are spelt incorrectly.

   b) Discuss the words you are not sure about with a partner and together work out whether they are spelt correctly.

   c) For each word that you have spelt incorrectly, work out what type of error it is.

Error type	Misspelling	Correct spelling
Homophones	I no we have the nicest garden. We have know mess after my brother moved out. knowbody	I know we have the nicest garden. We have no mess after my brother moved out. nobody
Verb forms	liveing, makeing, writeing	living, making, writing
Plurals	leave's, plant's, plate's, drink's	leaves, plants, plates, drinks
Word endings	beautifull, beautifuly, carefull, carefuly	beautiful → beautifully careful → carefully

3   Is there a pattern to the errors you have made that you can work out with your partner? Discuss how you could improve your spelling next time.

4   a) Look at your partner's piece of writing. Make a list of ten misspelt words in their work. You could use evidence from other pieces of writing as well. Then write down the correct spelling for each of these words, but don't let your partner see these yet. Use a dictionary to check you've got the correct spelling.

   b) Tell your partner one of the words he or she got wrong. First, ask him or her to guess the correct spelling of the word. If it is now right, ask him or her to guess how they spelt it originally. Take turns at the game until you've worked through both lists of misspelt words.

Extend your skills

Good spellers not only know the rules for certain words, but also have strategies to help them spell their problem words correctly.

1 Study this table of hints, strategies and tips to help you remember how to spell words correctly. Make a list of your ten problem words and pick a weapon of attack from the table to deal with each of them. You should then find that your problem words are really easy to spell.

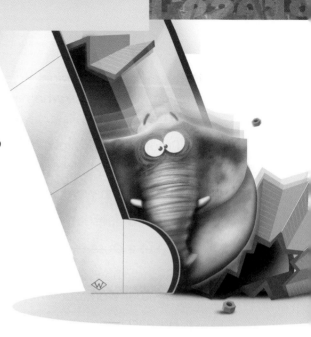

Weapon of attack	How it works	Examples
Mnemonic – this weapon helps you to remember the pattern	Make fun of your problem word by coming up with a phrase made up of words whose first letters spell out the word you want to remember.	because – <u>B</u>ig <u>E</u>lephants <u>C</u>an't <u>A</u>lways <u>U</u>se <u>S</u>mall <u>E</u>scalators ne<u>cess</u>ary – one collar and two sleeves.
Word within words	Attack the tough bits of your problem words by finding a way to remember the difficult part.	accelerate has 'celery' (almost!) in it separate has 'a rat' in it
Visualising	Make links between images and sequences of letters in your problem words.	desiccated (which is a very troublesome word!) can be remembered because it has the same letters as coconuts – s c c – just backwards! Since desiccated is a word we use with desiccated coconut, it's easy to remember.
Learning the root of the word	Find out the source of your problem word's power by finding out where its spelling comes from.	'celer' means swift or fast in Latin, which is why accelerate means 'get faster'.
Knowing word families	Know what word your problem word is related to, so you can knock them all out at once.	'Psyche' is the Greek mother of all words relating to the mind, like psychiatry, psychology, and psychic.

2 Now is your opportunity to let your teacher know what your ten problem words are, and how you've remembered them. You will need to write a couple of sentences for each of your words, explaining what the word is, what bit of it was difficult for you and how you attacked it. Here is an example:

> One of my problem words is 'opportunity'. I find that I often put 'oppurtunity' instead and I can never remember if it's 'o' or 'u' after the 'p'. I attacked it by finding a word within the word, which is 'port', and I imagined a traveller coming in to a port on a boat and seeing all the 'opportunity' in front of him.

3 Pick out the toughest problem word that you've really cracked. Design a poster to be used in class to illustrate how you cracked it and the weapon of attack you used against it.

4 Now look through a range of your writing, including your homework diary, exercise books from other subjects or work you have completed online. Check your spelling errors here and see if you need to add them to your problem word list. Eventually, your list will shrink as you attack each of them.

Apply your learning

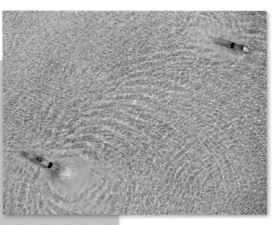

My dream home!

Some television programmes and magazines show houses that are out of this world. Now is your chance to do a bit of dreaming. Daydream Productions is advertising for people to submit their plans for their dream home. The most imaginative, detailed and creative entry will win a real-life version of their dream home!

Task

1 Write an entry for this competition explaining what your dream home would be like. Correct spelling will make a good impression on the judges, so you need to make sure that your writing doesn't include any errors. To make your entry stand out you will need to use some adventurous vocabulary, so be extra careful with these words.

2 Before you hand in your entry, make sure that you proofread it to identify any spelling errors. Use the strategies that you have learnt in this unit to check your work and correct any misspelt words.

Assess to Progress

1   Swap your work with a partner. Proofread your partner's work and see if you can find any spelling errors that they have not spotted. Give your partner feedback about any mistakes that you have identified.

2   Now rate yourself again from 1 to 7 for each of the skills below:

```
   1        2        3        4        5        6        7
```
I find this difficult.   I'm getting there.   I'm good at this.

- I can spot when words are spelt incorrectly, e.g. when an apostrophe is in the wrong place.

- I can spell most common words correctly, e.g. 'target' and 'learning'.

- I can spell more complicated words correctly, e.g. words like 'exaggerate' and 'strategy'.

- When I proofread and revise my writing, I check for spelling errors.

- I have a range of ways of learning how to spell words correctly, e.g. recording in a book or using spelling rules.

SKILLS FOR LIFE

Here are 33 spellings that people sometimes struggle with. In pairs, test each other and see how many you get right. Write down any words you struggle with and decide which method will help you learn to spell them correctly. Retest each other to see how far you have improved.

1. accommodation	12. business	23. fulfil
2. actually	13. caught	24. guard
3. although	14. concentration	25. happened
4. analyse	15. conscious	26. imaginary
5. argument	16. continuous	27. improvise
6. assessment	17. creation	28. industrial
7. autumn	18. evidence	29. interesting
8. beautiful	19. explanation	30. jealous
9. beginning	20. February	31. knowledge
10. believe	21. fierce	32. listening
11. buried	22. forty	33. lovely

Writing
Assessing your Progress

- Presenting a range of evidence fairly.
- Organising the points to help the reader understand.
- Giving a personal view.

Working through this unit will give you the opportunity to show the progress you have made in your writing skills. You will have the chance to bring together the skills you have developed in the earlier writing units as you prepare for a writing task that will assess how well you can write to comment.

Progress task:

Write a commentary on the litter situation in your neighbourhood, for inclusion in the school newspaper.

This is the task that you will complete at the end of the unit, but first let's find out what you already know about writing to comment.

Activate your learning

1   Working with a partner, look at the following features of writing to comment. Check that you understand the features by reading the explanations and think about which ones you use in your own writing.

- **Interesting opening and clear ending:** How can you get your reader hooked from the start? Good writers can make the ending strong by linking the ideas back to the introduction. What else makes a good ending?

- **Variety of sentence structures:** Beginning a sentence with an 'adverbial phrase' (i.e. an 'ly' word); using an 'embedded clause' (i.e. a clause added in the middle of a sentence). Embedded clauses will often be separated from the rest of the sentence by a pair of commas.

● **Topic structured into appropriate paragraphs:** Ideas need to be grouped together with a clear focus. What words that can be used to make links between paragraphs do you know?

● **Personal comment used to engage the reader:** Writing to comment means you can give some of your own views to help to keep the reader interested. Think about adding some asides where you are speaking directly to the reader.

● **Extreme responses shown through vocabulary choices, punctuation and grammar:** Effective writers choose vocabulary carefully and use punctuation to emphasise exactly what they mean.

2 Identify one feature that you think you can do well and one feature that is your target to improve.

Including these features in your writing will help you to be successful when writing to comment. Later in the unit you will look at a pupil's commentary on a different topic – school meals – and check whether these features have been included.

Build your ideas

Before you can start to write your commentary about litter in your neighbourhood, you need to collect some ideas about the topic of litter. Start by working in pairs to discuss the questions and comments about litter on the next page.

1 What are your views on each of them? Make notes to record your ideas.

2 When you have discussed each of the questions or statements, share your ideas with another pair and add their ideas to your notes.

Remember to make use of your ideas when you come to write your commentary at the end of the unit.

Campaigns: Do you remember any litter campaigns recently?

Do they work?

Fines: What fines are there for litter? Do they work? Is anyone ever caught?

Why do people throw litter out of car windows? Why can't they just throw it away when they get home?

More litter means more rats and foxes in our towns.

Chewing gum is worse than any litter. It should be banned.

Dog dirt: worst of all!
It is easy to clean up after your dog, so why don't people do it? Dog owners should be made to do community service if their dogs are caught fouling the streets.

Cigarette ends: Why can't people throw these away properly instead of throwing them on the ground or out of the car window?

Aren't people paid to do this?

Why should I do it? No one else does.

All this concern about litter on the streets is just a big fuss about nothing. Does it really matter?

Reinforce your learning

Now you are going to explore an example commentary about school meals that has been written by a pupil.

1   As you read, look for examples of the features of writing to comment that were listed in the Activate your learning section. Some features have already been pointed out for you.

> **Interesting opening. What makes it effective?**

It's official, at Goosegog High, school meals are 'OK!': we have enough time to eat them; there is lots of choice. This was the result of the survey we conducted, to find out about pupils' attitudes to the canteen and what it has to offer. However, the story is not as simple as at first it might appear from these general findings.

We interviewed 200 pupils across the years and 50 members of staff, in addition to sending questionnaires to parents. Opinions were varied and some were extreme. Because the pupils in the school all have different tastes and needs, there were some who did not have any food that they liked. Parents had an equally surprising range of thoughts about dinners. Some believed that there should be no choice, but others thought there was not enough. The cost of dinners was most commented on by parents, but there is a chance that children do not tell their parents the real cost, and keep the rest of the money! Most people, me included, think that the cost of the food is OK, except that chips are way over price! I know it's because we should pick the healthier options, which the canteen staff told me were kept cheap to encourage us, but now and again, it's nice to have a few chips. At the price they're sold at in our canteen, if you fancy a few chips, that's all you can afford!

The most popular meal was a surprise to me. I thought it would be pizza or burgers, but interestingly the most popular meal, by a long way, was Chinese noodles. It is a very tasty dish, and when it's on everyone gets excited. Honestly! Of course this means that it runs out soonest, especially with the teachers pushing in, but that's another issue to be mentioned later.

There were lots of ideas about how to make it healthier without making it boring. The best one came from a girl in Year 10 who says she is on a points diet. She thinks that the food should be given health points, so that you know how much food you have had that is bad for you in a week.

An example would be that chips and curry might have five points and green salad would have no points. Pupils could then add up the week in their planner, and know if they've gone through the health barrier of, for instance, 25 points. I thought this was a really good idea only if people were honest with themselves.

The Chip Shop Kids were most revealing as to why they do not go to the canteen. They do not like what is referred to as "healthy food" so go to the chip shop for cheaper and nicer versions of what is on sale in school. Unsurprisingly, the only suggestion they made as to how to persuade them to go back to the school choice was to decrease the price of the food and make more choices of fried food available. Their favourite dish, with vegetables nowhere to be seen, was always something and chips. The annoying thing was that these pupils were no fatter than anyone else. Life's unfair!

On complaints, number one from the pupils was pushing in by teachers and bigger kids. Teachers, however, were unhappiest about not being able to use salt! Surely, they could bring in their own and hide it in the staff room.

In conclusion, the school meal situation at our school is generally fine, and on the whole only needs a little changing to encourage the majority of pupils to eat healthier. Unless pupils are chained into their seats, it's not likely that those who go to the chip shop can be encourage to stay, however 'OK' the canteen is.

Sentence structure: Identify the embedded clause here. What effects does it create?

Sentence structure: This sentence begins with an adverbial phrase. What is the effect of this?

Extreme response shown through vocabulary and punctuation. How has the writer made this effective?

Personal comment to engage the reader. Explain the writer's attitude towards teachers.

Is this an effective conclusion? Explain why.

2 Working with a partner, reread the text and answer the annotated questions. Think carefully and try and explain how each example helps to create an effective commentary.

3 Create a table like the one below and find some more examples of the features of a commentary in this text. Try and explain what effect each one has.

Feature	Example	Effect
Variety of sentence structures: ● Beginning with adverbial phrases ● Embedding clauses	● ●	● ●
Personal comment used to engage the reader	●	●
Extreme responses shown through vocabulary choices, punctuation and grammar	●	●

Stretch

Which features of writing to comment do you think could have been used more often in this commentary? Are there any other writing features in this commentary that are effective?

4 Now think about how the commentary is structured. Working with a partner, carry out the following tasks to investigate the structure of the text:

a) Identify the main focus of each paragraph. How did you know?

b) Choose one paragraph and reread it carefully. Has the writer managed to make all of the sentences about the same topic? Are there any ideas that don't belong in the paragraph?

c) The conclusion is very clearly signalled to the reader. Are any other paragraphs signposted in this way? Can you think of any ways the writer could make clear links between the paragraphs?

Stretch

Look at paragraph 4. Describe how the writer has organised the ideas.
Then look at paragraph 2. How might this paragraph have been organised differently?

Progress task

You are now going to write your own commentary on litter. Start by revisiting the notes you made in the Build your ideas section. Then spend 10 minutes planning what you are going to write. Think about how to:

● present a range of evidence fairly

● organise the points to help the reader understand

● give a personal view.

You also need to make sure you think about how you are going to structure your commentary. You could use a plan like this:

Paragraphs	Outline of content
Intro	
Topic 1	
Topic 2	
Topic 3	
Conclusion	

Now write your commentary. You have got 40 minutes for this task.

Remember to:

● use your plan as you write

● include the features of writing to comment shown in the Activate your learning section and the example commentary on pages 223-224.

In the final 10 minutes, check the technical accuracy of your work (spelling, punctuation ... etc) and make sure that you have used the features in the checklist.

Assess to Progress

Read this pupil's commentary and then look at the annotations his teacher has provided.

Litter in my neighbourhood

Opening gets the reader hooked by listing types of litter.

Crisp packets, chocolate rappers, bottles, cartoons, cans, sweet rappers. These are just some of the things people throw down every day. Do you think it's right? I don't. In this report I will tell you the reasons why litter is wrong. I will cover from the town centre to corn bar.

Personal comment

Clear focus to the paragraph: the problem of litter. Points logically developed and in appropriate detail.

What is wrong with litter? Well it polutes the earth and it looks untidy. In some places it stinks and it can make you unwell. What's the point in throwing it everywhere when you can stick it in a bin. Round Corn Bar there are quite allot of bins, so there's not much rubbish, but up Corn Street there's hardly any bins atall, so it is quite untidy at times.

Adverbial phrase. You could have used it to start the sentence.

I mostly find that where no one cleans up rubbish, like the council, there's a lot of rubbish. Stuff made out of plastic and stuff arn't biodegradable, so if no one moves them they could be their for ages.

We need litter sorted out before it takes over our world. The solutions should be used every day.

Ends with solutions: another list. But it seems to end quite suddenly. What could you do to improve this?

- Put rubbish in a bin
- Recycle
- Pick up litter you see on the floor.
- Clean up after you and you dog.

Varied sentence structures: question and answer then a short sentence.

Makes the purpose clear

Vocabulary chosen for effect.

Rhetorical questions also used to engage the reader.

Embedded clause and phrase.

Embedded clause

Vocabulary chosen to emphasise point.

1 Although this pupil has shown some of the features of writing a commentary, not all of them have been used. Find parts of the response that you could rewrite to:

- begin with an adverbial phrase

- show extreme responses through punctuation

- give the commentary an effective ending.

2 a) Now swap work with a partner and annotate the features of writing a commentary that you find in their response. Find at least one feature that you think could be developed or improved and explain how they could do this.

b) When you get your own work back, look at the annotations. Add to the notes if you think there are any features that you think your partner has missed. Then read their advice carefully and have a go at what they have suggested.

3 Look back at the list of features of writing to comment and review your progress. Which ones do you now feel most confident about? Which do you still need to work on? What would you do to improve your writing next time?

Pearson Education
Edinburgh Gate
Harlow
Essex
CM20 2JE
© Pearson Education Limited 2008

Series Editor: Geoff Barton
Series Consultant: Michael Jones

The rights of Geoff Barton, Bernadette Carroll, Clare Constant, Emma Lee, Michele Paule and Alan Pearce to be identified as the authors of this work has been asserted by them in accordance with the Copyright, Design and Patents Act of 1988.

With many thanks to Chris Edge and John Green.

ISBN: 978-1-4058-7516-5

We are grateful to the following for permission to reproduce copyright material and photographs:

Aha! Jokes for an extract from 'Do you want children?' published on http://www.AhaJokes.com/; Amazon.co.uk for a review of *Harry Potter and the Order of the Phoenix* DVD published on www.amazon.co.uk; Andersen Press Ltd for an extract and illustrations from *Super Dooper Jezebel* by Tony Ross published by Picture Lions 1989, ISBN 978-0006631507; AP Watt Ltd for an extract from *The Red Room* by HG Wells reproduced by permission of AP Watt Ltd on behalf of The Literary Executors of the Estate of H G Wells; BBC for a transcript from the *Ten O'clock News* bulletin TX:22/01/2007 © BBC, 2007; BBC for a transcript from a BBC School Television programme *Writer's Block* © BBC, 2007; BBC for a screenshot from www.bbc.co.uk/parenting/your_kids/teen_appreciate.shtml and the transcript from "Beach Bonanza" copyright © BBC, reproduced with permission; Caroline Sheldon Literary Agency for the poem "Windrush Child" by John Agard copyright © 1998 by John Agard reproduced by kind permission of John Agard c/o Caroline Sheldon Literary Agency Limited; Crazyaboutgadgets for a screenshot from www.crazyaboutgadgets.com copyright © Crazyaboutgadgets.com, reproduced with permission; Eddison Pearson Ltd for the poem "Tables" from *Duppy Jamboree* by Valerie Bloom copyright © 1992 Valerie Bloom, reprinted by permission of Valerie Bloom; Global Ethics for details about One Water from http://www.onewater.org.uk; Islamic Relief Worldwide for an extract from "Orphaned by the Tsunami" published on www.islamic-relief.com, reproduced with permission; Jamie Oliver Limited for an extract from "Jamie Oliver's Manifesto for School Dinners" published on www.jamieoliver.com copyright © Jamie Oliver Limited; Lexis PR for screenshot details from a journey plan on www.thetrainline.com; Little, Brown Book Group Limited and Curtis Brown for Grace Nichols poem 'Praise Song for My Mother' Copyright © Grace Nichols 1984 reproduced with permission of Little, Brown Book Group Ltd and Curtis Brown Group Ltd; Mirrorpix for the article "Teen paid to play games" by Richard Smith published in *The Mirror* 11th October 2007 copyright © Mirrorpix 2007; The Orion Publishing Group Ltd and Abner Stein for an extract adapted from *Miracle in the Andes: 72 Days on the Mountain and my Long Trek Home* by Nando Perrado published by Orion Non-Fiction, an imprint of The Orion Publishing Group; Oxfam Education & Youth for a screenshot from http://www.oxfam.org.uk" www.oxfam.org.uk/coolplanet/kidsweb/fairtrade/fairtrade3.htm with the permission of Oxfam GB, Oxfam House, John Smith Drive, Cowley, Oxford OX4 2JY, UK www.oxfam.org.uk/education. Oxfam GB does not necessarily endorse any text or activities that accompany the materials; PFD for the poems "I love me mudder" from *The Bloomsbury Book of Love Poems* by Benjamin Zephaniah copyright © 2001 Benjamin Zephaniah and "Childhood Tracks" from *Only One of Me* by James Berry copyright © 2004 James Berry, reproduced by permission of PFD www.pfd.co.uk on behalf of Benjamin Zephaniah and James Berry; Princeton University Press for the illustrations 'drug-free spider's web', 'effect of caffeine' and 'effect of marijuana' published in *Spider Communication* by Peter N Witt copyright © Princeton University Press 1982. Reprinted by permission; The Rod Hall Agency Limited for the poem 'Kidspoem/Bairnsang' by Liz Lochhead reproduced by permission of The Rod Hall Agency on behalf of Liz Lochead; Simply Travel for a screenshot from www.simplytravel.co.uk © copyright TUI UK Limited 2008. Simply Travel is a division of TUI UK Limited; Telegraph Media Group Limited for an extract from "Revealed: Titanic was doomed before it set sail" by Jasper Copping published in *The Telegraph* 10th June 2007 copyright © The Telegraph 2007; Timbertops Animal Agency for material from http://animalagency.co.uk/index.html; Time Out, London for an extract from "The Science of Spying" by John O'Connell published on www.timeout.com issue 1904, 14th-20th February 2007 copyright © Time Out, London 2007 reproduced courtesy of Time Out London; UK Fire Service Resources for a screenshot from www.fireservice.co.uk copyright © 2008 UK Fire Service Resources, reprinted with permission; Walker Books Limited for extracts from Raven's Gate by Anthony Horowitz copyright © Anthony Horowitz 2005, and "As You Like It" from *Bravo, Mr. William Shakespeare* by Marcia Williams reproduced by permission of Walker Books Ltd, London SE11 5HJ; and WWF-UK for two screenshots from www.panda.org copyright © WWF-UK, reproduced with permission.

Photographs:

(Key: b-bottom; c-centre; l-left; r-right; t-top)

Alamy Images: Andrew Fox 232; Andrew Wakeford 118tr; Chris Howes/Wild Places Photography 226; Colin Underhill / Alamy 237; David Martyn Hughes 12b; Dennis Hallinan 219; Gari Wyn Williams 50-51; Gary Roebuck 209; Israel images 95t; Joanne Moyes 18; Matthias Engelien 78b; Peter Barritt 217; Profimedia International s.r.o. 94; Stephen Frink Collection 108; The Print Collector 180; Corbis: Anuruddha Lokuhapuarachchi 174; Bettmann 124, 172; Corbis 89; Michael Kevin Daly 69; Dex Images 94b; Image Plus 221; John Edward Linden 223; Ralph White 171; Getty Images: Brad Wilson 17; Bruce Laurance 118bl; Cambridge Jones 130; Chris Jackson 52;

David Aubrey 114; David Deas 3; Dorling Kindersley 119b; Evan Agostini 47; Gerry Cranham/Time & Life Pictures 95b; Getty Images 8l; Ian Mckinnell 77; Jon Feingersh 165; Juan Mabromata 164; Joe McBride 48–49; Paul Thomas 14; Peter Hince 79; Ryan McVay 28; Susanna Price 119t; Todd Warnock 78t; Wides & Holl 101; Yellow Dog Productions 146; Zac Macaulay 104-105; Image Quest Marine: Carlos Villoch 111; iStockphoto: 33, 91; Kobal Collection Ltd: BROADWAY PICTURES / THE KOBAL COLLECTION / GREENE, BOB 193; Live Alchemy: 196; Panos Pictures: Giacomo Pirozzi 16; Pearson Education Ltd: 71c; Photolibrary.com: 8r; Photolibrary.com 94tl (1), 104; 127; PunchStock: 94tr (2), 118br, 118tl; Bananastock 23, 94 (3); Comstock images 60-61; Creatas Images 78c; Punchstock 71l; Reuters: Luke MacGregor 12c; Stephen Hird 12t; Rex Features: Jonathan Hordle 185; Patrick Frilet 158-159; Science & Society Picture Library: Science & Society Picture Library 131, 132; Writer Pictures: 125; Ken Wilson-Max; 7b, 15b, 23b, 31b, 37b, 45b, 69b, 81, 93, 103, 113, 123, 133b, 155, 167, 177, 189, 198, 207, 216, 224b

Cover Image: Getty Images: Angelo Cavalli/Iconica/

All other images © Pearson Education

Picture Research by: Sally Cole

Illustrations provided by:

Dan Chernett, pages 4 and 5; Bee Willey, page 6; Chris Gould, pages 27 and 30; Bob Doucet, page 39; Lucien Gorlier, page 42; Bee Willey, page 64; Darren Phillips-Boyd, pages 67 and 73; Lucien Gorlier, page 82; Bob Doucet, page 86; Lucien Gorlier, page 97; Darren Phillips-Boyd, pages 101, 103 and 121; Bob Doucet, pages 136, 137, 138, 189 and 140; Darren Phillips-Botd, page 143; Tohe Eriksen, page 162; Dan Chernett, page 169; Mike Spoor, page 183; Dan Chernett, page 186; Ruth Palmer, page 194; Lucien Gorlier, page 203; Dan Chernett, pages 205 and 206; Bee Willey, page 216; Vincent Viglo, page 227.

Printed and bound in Great Britain at Scotprint, Haddington.

Every effort has been made to trace copyright holders and we apologise in advance for any unintentional omissions. We would be pleased to insert the appropriate acknowledgement in any subsequent edition of this publication.